How to Write an Essay Like an Equation:

Write Better, Easier, Faster

Second Edition

Eric Sentell, PhD

ericsentell.medium.com

<u>Sign-up for Eric's Newsletter</u>

Also by Eric Sentell:

<u>Become Your Own Fact-Checker:
Know Who's Misleading and Manipulating
You</u>

HOW TO WRITE AN ESSAY LIKE AN EQUATION

Copyright © 2020 by Eric Sentell.

For information contact :

Eric Sentell

http://www.ericsentell.com

Book and Cover design by Eric Sentell

Cover designed with Canva

First Edition: March 2020

Second Edition: January 2021

Table of Contents

Introduction

A friend of mine said he hated English and writing because they are so subjective. He said this to me, an English and writing teacher. Not exactly audience-aware, was he?

He added, "I like math because there's one right answer. English isn't like that. There are multiple answers and exceptions to everything. I hate it."

At the time of this conversation, I had a PhD in English and a decade of experience teaching writing at universities and community colleges. I didn't want to get into a debate with my friend at that moment, but I thought to myself ....

... writing isn't nearly as subjective as most people think. An essay can be quite similar to an algebra equation in terms of development and structure. Obviously, their structures are vastly different, but both an essay and an equation can be highly systematic in how they are created.

The more I thought about that conversation, about past students who disliked English, and about popular misconceptions of writing, the more I realized there were many people who could benefit from learning how to write an essay like an equation.

Then I also realized that all those people had been left in the wilderness.

Pick up any book about writing, for any ability level, and you will find a labyrinth of long chapters presenting multiple options when one option would do, digging into every nuance when straightforward explanations would be better, and offering cumbersome examples that poorly fit the needs of most writers.

Writing courses are expensive and variable in quality. Even at a community college, tuition costs hundreds of dollars per credit hour. A course is only as good as its instructor, but even the best instructors often shy away from the "right answers" that many people want. In the classroom, our goal is to develop critical thinking and problem solving.

By teaching you to write like you're doing math, I hope to help you thrive in an economy in which 97% of business executives rank writing as "very important." And I also hope you will join the many students who have confessed in their course evaluations, "I used to hate writing, but thanks to Dr. Sentell, I actually like it now."

In the chapters that follow, I will cover only the essentials of writing with only the necessary amount of detail and explanation. This is not a book for creative writers. This is a book for busy people who need practical, straight-forward solutions to the challenges of written communication:

- ❑ people who need to write better at work;
- ❑ students who struggle with writing;
- ❑ students in programs whose professors don't (or can't) teach writing;
- ❑ students preparing for college entrance exams;
- ❑ international students who need to prepare for Western or American writing;
- ❑ high school teachers preparing students for college;
- ❑ home-schooling parents who want to provide excellent instruction; and
- ❑ anyone who craves the "one right answers" of writing.

I have honed the "one right answer" to each of writing's essentials during a decade-plus of learning what student-writers need to know and how to teach it most effectively. In this book, you will learn about the following crucial components of academic and professional writing:

- ❑ Audience
- ❑ Purpose
- ❑ Genre
- ❑ The BLUF
- ❑ PEE Paragraph Structure
- ❑ Content-Lexical Ties
- ❑ The Paramedic Method of Editing
- ❑ Sentence Boundaries
- ❑ A Practical Style Guide
- ❑ Diction
- ❑ The Writing Process

I will explain, define, and describe each concept, present strategies and examples of their use, and offer thought-exercises and writing activities to reinforce and build on what you learn.

Let's begin with the paramount concept of writing.

1

Audience

Audience is simple and complex. It is the person or group to whom you're writing. Simple, right? But who is this person really? How do you figure out how to communicate to them most clearly and persuasively? Complex, isn't it?

Reflect on almost any argument with a parent, sibling, spouse, or friend and you'll quickly recognize how difficult it can be to communicate clearly even when, theoretically, you know the audience very well. You will also recognize the paramount importance of audience-awareness.

Fortunately, we can bridge the simplicity and complexity of audience.

Concrete and Imagined Audiences

According to the influential writing theorists Lisa Ede and Andrea Lunsford, every piece of writing has a "concrete audience" and an "imagined audience."

A concrete audience exists in the physical world. It is the physical reader who will receive and read your writing. You could walk up to the concrete audience and hand them printed pages. You might even personally know the person or people in your concrete audience. Whether you are friends with the concrete audience or have never met them, you can learn a great deal about the audience with a little research, reading, and thinking.

An imagined audience exists in the writer's imagination. It is the writer's idea of the reader who will receive and read the writing. Writers can't walk up to the imagined audience, even though they might personally know the people they are imagining. Through your writing, your words, you will "bring to life" the audience that you imagine.

Every piece of writing, every writer, has both a concrete audience and an imagined audience at the same time. There are always concrete, physical readers. But when we sit down to write, those readers are seldom standing over our shoulders and asking questions or giving feedback. When we write, we must imagine the concrete audience to whom we are writing. As we write to them, we use certain content, style, tone, phrases, or words that connect with them. The more we connect with them, the more we bring them to life.

As I write this book, for example, I know there are people in the world who want the perspective on writing that I am attempting to provide. But since I'm sitting alone at my desk, I must imagine those people and their experiences, emotions, needs, desires, and goals. I am striving to keep the content short and to the point. I am using a conversational tone. If I were writing for a concrete audience of Composition and Rhetoric scholars, then I would imagine a very different kind of audience and I would write very differently as a result.

Here's another example. Think about your favorite hobby, recreation, or entertainment. Next, think about someone who shares your passion for it. Then imagine a conversation with that person. What, specifically, would you talk about? What would be of mutual interest? How would you talk about it?

Now, imagine discussing the same subject with someone who knows nothing about it. How would you explain it to that person? How would the conversation's content change? How would its tone and style change? How would you get this audience to be interested in the topic?

In each of these examples, there is a concrete audience that exists in the physical world. You can learn about this audience through interacting with them. There is an imagined audience that the writer builds in his or her mind, a mental model if you will. Writers try to engage the imagined audience so that they can communicate effectively to the concrete audience.

Multiple Audiences

Following Ede and Lunsford's lead, writing researcher Mary Jo Reiff argued that writers have multiple audiences. Where Ede and Lunsford suggested that a single audience could be simultaneously concrete and imagined, Reiff pointed out that beyond the classroom most writers have multiple audiences. Each of these audiences is both concrete and imagined.

For instance, I am aware of multiple audiences as I write this book:

❑ adults who write for their jobs and recognize the necessity of improving, or at least better tolerating, their writing;

- ❏ college students who are well into their majors, struggling with writing, and learning from professors who are subject-matter experts but not writing teachers;
- ❏ college students who are just beginning classes and need to pass the required writing courses;
- ❏ high school teachers who want a concise book to help prepare their students for college entrance exams and courses; and
- ❏ home-schooling parents who lack subject-matter expertise but want to instill effective writing abilities.

Each audience is a concrete group, and I am imagining each as I write.

Above, I wrote, "Think about your favorite hobby, recreation, or entertainment." But originally I wrote, "Think about someone with whom you work, take classes, share a favorite school subject, or share a hobby." In the original, I was trying to appeal to all of my multiple audiences simultaneously. In the revision, I still appeal to all of my audiences (who doesn't have a favorite hobby, recreation, or entertainment?) but I appeal to them more concisely.

Here's another example. Your boss asks you to write a flyer promoting a customer appreciation party. Who is your audience? The customers? Your boss? Your co-workers?

Your audience includes all of them. Your primary audience are the customers. Your purpose is to inform the customers about the party and encourage them to attend. But your boss is a secondary audience. The boss will want the flyer to represent the company positively, another purpose.

A shocking image and some provocative writing might grab the customers' attention, achieving the purpose of informing the primary audience about the party, but it will not achieve the boss's additional purpose of maintaining the company's image. You must keep in mind both audiences and try to satisfy both of their needs.

Then there are your coworkers, who will surely use the flyer's information to promote the event to customers. They will need to know the key details (time and location) as well as the selling points (food? games? prizes?).

We haven't even mentioned the potential audiences who might happen to see the flyer wherever it's posted, even though you may not have any intention of non-customers seeing the flyer or coming to the party.

Developing Audience-Awareness

To recap, every piece of writing has multiple audiences, and each audience is both concrete (a physical entity) and imagined (a mental model).

How can you develop awareness of each audience, so that you can communicate effectively to all of them at once?

Remember that each audience is concrete; therefore, you can learn about each audience through some simple interactions.

You may have already interacted with the audience more than you realize. Presumably, you will have interacted with customers and your boss before being asked to write a customer appreciation party flyer. You already know these audiences through your experiences with them. You have taken classes in history, biology, chemistry, economics, and more. So you already know the audiences of historians, biologists, chemists, economists, and academics in general by having observed, heard, and interacted with them.

Let's say you have never interacted with a concrete audience. You were hired yesterday and already you are being asked to write a flyer for the customer appreciation party. Or you have never taken a class in fluid dynamics. Or you have never read Wired magazine (you're missing out!).

How do you learn about audiences with whom you have never interacted? Research and read. Locate information about, for, or by the audience, and then consume that information.

Maybe you ask your new coworkers about the customers, the boss, or both. Perhaps you call a few customers to ask what they would like to do at the party. If there is a flyer from last year's party, then you could study how it tries to appeal to the customers, boss, and coworkers and then model your flyer after it. Best of all, you can ask some customers, coworkers, and the boss for feedback on your draft.

You could check out a book on fluid dynamics and look up some articles in trade magazines or scholarly journals. By reading this material, you will learn about fluid dynamics, but you should also observe how the material is written by and for the audience of fluid dynamics research. You can observe how the authors write about the subject, which will give you a model and also reveal the audience's knowledge, experience, and expectations. If you can find an expert on fluid dynamics, you could get input from that person on your writing.

You can start reading some articles in Wired, noting what types of topics the magazine covers, what level of detail the articles provide, how much jargon they use, what assumptions they make about the audience's interests, education, or expertise. You can read the magazine's "About" page and other promotional materials to get a sense of how the magazine conceives of itself and its readers. You can find a reader of Wired, ask for feedback on the article you want to submit, and use that feedback to improve it.

In short, you can learn a lot about a concrete audience through a couple simple strategies:

- ❑ reflecting on your interactions with them;
- ❑ reading what they write and read;
- ❑ noticing how they write what they read; and
- ❑ getting feedback if possible.

Once you know more about your audience, you can imagine the audience while you write or revise your draft. You can put yourself in the reader's shoes and try to view your writing from their perspective. You can anticipate where they might be confused, when they might have questions that need answered, or when they might object to what you're saying.

You can also anticipate important expectations, needs, or goals for the audience:

- ❑ what the audience knows about the subject;
- ❑ what the audience does not know about it;

- ❑ what the audience will find inherently interesting;
- ❑ what the audience will need to be convinced is interesting or relevant;
- ❑ what information will help the audience achieve its goals in reading;
- ❑ what information will convince the audience of your main idea (or thesis); and
- ❑ what kind of tone would be most engaging or appropriate.

When you can anticipate these and other needs of your multiple audiences, then you have audience-awareness. Audience-awareness is crucial to effective writing.

Where Does It Fit in the Equation?

Audience is the paramount consideration of writing. Writing can be extraordinary, but if it lacks audience-awareness, it will not communicate effectively.

Our writing equation begins as follows:

Audience-Awareness + …

To develop audience-awareness, first understand the nature of audience. It is concrete and thus knowable. It is imagined and thus a mental model. It consists of multiple people or groups, who may have different and competing expectations, needs, or goals. You learn about the audience through interaction, observation, reading, reflection, and feedback.

Once you learn about the audience, you will be able to write with audience-awareness. You can anticipate confusions, questions, or objections as well as expectations, needs, and goals. You may anticipate these things while drafting, while rewriting your draft, or both.

Here are some thought-exercises and activities to hone your audience-awareness.

Thought-Exercises

Honestly, how often do we actually do the exercises at the end of the chapter unless a teacher makes us? Thought-exercises are much more likely to actually be completed, and you can do them anywhere and anytime.

1. Imagine a shelf of magazines at a grocery store's checkout register. Based on the covers alone, who is the target audience for each magazine? How do you know this?

2. Think about the last thing you read. Who was the intended audience? What features in the writing make the audience clear?

3. Still contemplating the last thing you read, think about the opposite of the intended audience. How would the writing need to change for this audience?

4. Suppose you were asked to explain a major holiday to each of the following audiences in a way that would be most relevant and interesting.

    a. Historians

    b. Economists

    c. Psychologists

    d. Writers

    e. Military personnel

    f. Postal workers (or mail carriers)

    g. How would you change your explanation based on each audience? Why would you change it in these specific ways? How did you know how to adapt to each audience?

Activities

But of course, sometimes you want to test out your skills. For writing, this means actually writing. Try the following writing activity to practice and develop your audience-awareness.

1. Choose an article you read or your own piece of writing. Revise that article so that it engages a different audience than originally intended or targeted.

2. Write explanations of a major holiday to each of the audiences listed above. What information do you provide or emphasize? What level of detail and tone do you use?

3. Choose a piece of writing that you did for work or school. List the number of potential audiences who might read it, both the intended (or primary) audience and the unintended (or additional) audiences. Explain in writing how each audience might react to or perceive the writing and how you can balance each audience's needs.

2

Purpose

Purpose is the reason why you write to the audience. It is also the reason why your audience should care about what you write. Only audience matters more than purpose.

There are many possible purposes for writing. Novelists, poets, and memoirists entertain. Pretty much everyone else informs or persuades in some way. We will focus on informative and persuasive purposes, including some common variations thereof.

Your purpose should serve the expectations, needs, or goals of the audience. In other words, your writing should help the audience meet a need, achieve a goal, or take an action.

If the reader does not see the purpose behind what you write, then the reader will struggle to care about it. Readers are always wondering,

- ❏ So what?
- ❏ Why should I care?
- ❏ What will I get out of this?
- ❏ Will this meet my needs, achieve my goals, or enable an action I (may) want to take?

You must establish a sense of purpose, either directly or indirectly, to keep the reader's attention and interest.

Types of Purposes

Every piece of nonfiction provides information. It may be purely informative in purpose, or it may have an emphasis in its purpose, such as analysis, evaluation, or persuasion.

Usually, the writing task will give you some clues about your purpose. If a history teacher asks for an essay "comparing" the Civil Rights Movement and the Women's Rights Movement, then you know what purpose, needs, or goals your audience expects you to achieve.

Here are some of the more common purposes in nonfiction writing, the words that typically describe them, and brief explanations of those terms:

- ❏ Informative / Inform
    - ❏ provide information and ideas
- ❏ let readers make up their own minds
    - ❏ Persuasive / Persuade
- ❏ provide information and ideas
    - ❏ convince readers to agree with your positions
- ❏ Analysis / Analyze
    - ❏ break down information and ideas
    - ❏ explain what things mean or why they matter
- ❏ Evaluation / Evaluate
    - ❏ assess information and ideas
    - ❏ explain what makes something good, bad, or both
- ❏ Comparison / Compare / Compare and Contrast
    - ❏ compare information and ideas
    - ❏ explain similarities and differences
    - ❏ clarify what makes something distinctive (or not distinctive)
- ❏ Definition / Define
    - ❏ define a complex idea, concept, or problem
    - ❏ explain the nature of something

- ❏ Description / Describe
  - ❏ describe something physically, emotionally, or both
  - ❏ describe events as they happened
  - ❏ the who, what, when, where, how, and why
- ❏ Process / Explain
  - ❏ outline and explain the process of doing something (a "how-to")

Sometimes, writing may have multiple purposes. The report on the Space Shuttle Challenger explosion, for example, described what happened that led to the explosion, analyzed the information about the events, and explained how the process of space shuttle launches could be improved. This explanation was partly informative and partly persuasive.

The flyer promoting a customer appreciation party will inform customers about the party and its details, persuade them to attend the party, promote a positive image of the company, persuade customers to stay loyal to the company, and help coworkers tell customers about the party.

Whatever your purposes, you will provide information that helps the audience achieve a goal, meet a need, or take an action.

Establishing Purpose

It bears repeating: you must establish a sense of purpose, either directly or indirectly, to keep the reader's attention and interest.

But how do you establish purpose?

First, state your purpose early in whatever you are writing. A murder mystery novel shouldn't reveal the murderer until near the end, but most informative writing needs to get to the point quickly before readers decides this piece of writing is not meeting their informational needs.

Second, state your purpose explicitly. Tell readers what you want them to know and why. Don't merely hint at it.

Third, use specific language, including the language of the writing task. The more specific and detailed your language, the more clearly you will express your purpose and main idea. Borrow from the prompt or the request from your audience.

Fourth, draft and rewrite. As I will discuss more fully in the chapters on thesis statements and the writing process, sometimes you need to write a draft to figure out what you think about a topic.

Then you can rewrite the draft to highlight or emphasize your purpose early in the writing, explicitly, and with specific language.

Examples of Establishing Purpose

When your history teacher asks you to "compare" and "evaluate" the Civil Rights Movement and the Women's Rights Movement, then you could begin your paper with something like the following:

> ❏ "The Civil Rights Movement and the Women's Rights Movement have many similarities but also important differences. Both movements had charismatic and influential leaders, tireless organizers, and large groups of supporters throughout the country. Yet the Civil Rights Movement achieved more victories through landmark court cases, while the Women's Rights Movement created more change in social norms and attitudes. The latter had a greater and longer-lasting impact."

In this example, I did not "hit the reader over the head" with awkward phrases like, "I will compare the Civil Rights and Women's Rights Movements" or "After evaluating both movements, I have concluded …."

But I still stated a clear purpose early in the paper, using explicit and specific language as well as borrowing from the task or prompt provided by the audience. It is very clear that I am comparing these movements and evaluating them, thanks to language like "similarities" and "differences," comparisons of specific achievements and methods, and an evaluation of each movement's impact.

Notice that my evaluation is subtly persuasive. Reasonable people could disagree with my evaluation. Thus, I need to write a paper developing the evaluation and convincing readers to agree with it, and the audience needs to read the paper to decide whether they agree or disagree. Conflict creates interest.

A strong sense of purpose often has a subtle persuasive element, or conflict or tension.

When your boss asks you to write the customer appreciation flyer, then you could write something like this in large, colorful font:

- ❑ "You're invited! Stress-Free Tax Prep will host a Customer Appreciation Party at its main office, May 1st at 12:00 pm, to thank you for your business and celebrate another stress-free tax season. Join us for BBQ, drinks, door prizes, and fun games for the family."

In this example, the primary purpose could not be clearer. Customers are invited in the first sentence. The secondary purpose, persuading them to actually attend, also comes across in the promised incentives. Notice that door prizes will entice adults while the games will encourage them to bring their children, taking care of the potential obstacle of finding childcare.

The purpose of promoting a positive image also comes across, satisfying the boss's goals. Thanking the customers indicates gratitude, a trait that reflects positively on the company. Referring to "another stress-free tax season" reminds customers of the service and value that the company provides. This reminder will encourage continued loyalty to the company even if customers skip the party.

Coworkers also have their purposes served. The "when and where" information and the incentives provide the details that coworkers will need to encourage customers to attend.

It is helpful to focus on one audience and purpose at a time, especially while coming up with ideas and writing a first draft. After you have something down on paper (or a computer screen), then you can begin to think about other audiences and purposes and how to make sure you are also serving those needs.

Where Does It Fit in the Equation?

You might feel overwhelmed thinking about meeting the needs of multiple audiences and serving multiple purposes all at the same time. But this task can be approached systematically:

- ❑ learn about your audiences (see chapter one);
- ❑ put yourself in their shoes (one pair at a time!);
- ❑ consider their needs and goals;
- ❑ consider what actions you would like the audience to take; and
- ❑ establish a purpose that serves those needs and goals or enables those actions.

To establish purpose:

- ❑ state your purpose early;
- ❑ state your purpose explicitly;
- ❑ use specific language;
- ❑ draft and rewrite;
- ❑ make sure your purpose comes across clearly

One might add to our writing equation as follows:

Audience-Awareness + Purpose + ….

When you combine audience-awareness with a sense of purpose, your writing will become far more effective.

Here are some thought-exercises and activities to build your understanding of purpose and your ability to express it in an engaging way.

Thought-Exercises

1. Think of the last thing you read. What was its purpose? How did the writing make its purpose clear? What did the writer say? Where did the writer say it?

2. Think about the various sections of a newspaper, magazine, or news website. How many different purposes are served or achieved? How is each purpose made clear to the reader? How does the writing change from one section to the next based on its purpose?

3. Suppose you need to have an important conversation with someone. How would you make your purpose in the conversation as clear to that person as possible from the beginning of the conversation?

Activities

1. Write out your opening in the important conversation mentioned earlier. Make your purpose as clear and engaging as possible. Make it relevant and interesting to your audience.

2. Choose a piece of writing that you did for work or school. Read through it. What was your purpose? How did your writing achieve it? Do you need to make your purpose clearer, or focus more on achieving it? If so, how?

3. Write an introduction paragraph that grabs the reader's attention through some surprising or very practical information and then states your purpose in the rest of the writing. It may or may not be directly related to the surprising or practical information.

3

Genre

Purpose is closely connected to genre. A genre is a type of writing (or movie, music, art, etc.) that has some standard conventions, characteristics, or features. Poetry is distinct from short stories, and short stories are not research papers. A Western movie would never be confused with a Sci-Fi film — unless the movie blends genres like Cowboys and Aliens.

A given genre has a purpose. A novel entertains. A research paper synthesizes information from multiple sources into a cohesive discussion. An incident report summarizes the details of what happened, who was involved, and what steps were taken next.

Readers expect a new piece of writing within a given genre to have the same or similar characteristics as previous pieces they have read within that genre. When they pick up a thriller novel, they expect a fast-paced plot with high stakes because other thrillers have those elements. When they sit down with an incident report, they expect a clear, organized narrative of events — the who, what, where, when, how, and why — because previous incident reports offered that kind of information and detail.

Why did the previous incident reports offer that information and detail? Because previous incident report readers needed it.

As discussed in earlier chapters, audiences have needs and goals. Establishing purpose shows audiences that your writing will meet those needs and goals.

When enough people have the same needs and goals, then writers meet those needs and goals often enough for a genre to form. Genres have certain characteristics because those specific features serve the audience's needs more effectively than other features would.

A thriller novel has a fast-paced plot and high stakes because it entertains a certain kind of reader more than a slow-paced plot without earth-shaking consequences riding on the outcome. An incident report contains certain information and details because readers can't understand the incident without them.

When the audience expects your writing to fit within a certain genre, then they will be confused and frustrated when it does not have the expected characteristics. The audience requested or selected that genre in order to meet a need, achieve a goal, or enable an action.

Your writing does not serve the audience's purpose if it lacks the specific features of the genre they requested or selected. If they had different needs or goals, they would have chosen a different genre.

If you click on an article titled, "20 Hilarious Things from the 90s that No One Remembers," then you expect entertainment, humor, and nostalgia presented through a numbered list, pictures, and short paragraphs with punch-lines. Another genre of article might also meet these needs, but it won't meet them the same way. A lengthy essay consisting of long, rambling paragraphs would violate your expectations for the genre indicated by the title.

If you click on an article with a title like, "New Legislation May Impact Gas Prices," then you expect an informative report about the new legislation and how it might increase or decrease gas prices, thus affecting your transportation and pocketbook. You would be surprised by arguments for or against the legislation and a "call-to-action" to contact your Congressional representatives. You might then question the accuracy of the information since the article clearly has an agenda, unlike most news reports.

If you see an article titled, "Oil Refinery Law Helps Big Oil, Hurts Consumers," then you would expect a persuasive essay arguing against the new law and attacking the legislators who passed it, the Big Oil lobbyists who helped pass it, and the general unfairness of the system. This expectation would be especially strong if the title were preceded by "Opinion," a marker for distinguishing an opinion-editorial from a news report. You would be frustrated if the article offered only straight-forward news reporting without any interpretation or analysis like you expected.

You must keep the genre in mind when you write so that you can anticipate the reader's expectations, needs, and goals and then serve those purposes through the genre's conventions.

Learning New Genres

You learn new genres by reading those genres. If you seek out examples and read them effectively, then you don't need to be taught each and every genre that you might encounter.

But you must read the examples like a writer, not a reader. You should not read just for content or comprehension. You should also pay attention to how the content is presented. How is it organized? What information is placed here, and what is there? What kind of information is provided? What kind of style or tone is used?

Let's say an author writes a lengthy article about his or her small rural hometown, interviews many farmers and ranchers and former factory workers, and tells their stories of struggle in the new knowledge-based economy. The article begins with a particular farmer's story, shares the author's personal connection, zooms out to discuss the whole town's situation, and then shares a series of other people's stories that illustrate the town's situation. There are a few numbers and statistics, but the author mostly focuses on the people and their stories. You are reading "long-form journalism," or narrative-based reporting with strong human interest.

Another author writes an analysis of the impact on rural communities of global supply chains, trends in automation and outsourcing, increasing self-sufficiency in developing economies, and free trade policies. The article begins with statistics about the plight of small towns, presents graphs and tables summarizing the data, and connects the numbers to the business and governmental policies of the last forty years. Then you are reading a very different genre of article about more-or-less the same topic.

By paying attention to the type of information provided and its organization, you can get a good sense of the genre. Seek out examples, and read them like a writer.

For example, I had never written software documentation, but I needed to understand the genre. With just a few minutes on Google, I found several examples of software documentation. I read them for the type of information they provided, how they organized the information, the amount of detail they provided, and their style and tone.

I quickly learned that software documentation includes a table-of-contents, an introduction, and sections like "general design constraints," "functional requirements," "nonfunctional requirements," "system architecture," "server architecture," and more. They use headings to organize the information, and the writing is terse and to-the-point.

Examples of Genres

There are a multitude of genres of writing. No book can teach them all. But here are some common genes whose characteristics often apply across multiple other genres:

- ❑ Research Paper
- ❑ Report

- ❑ Analysis / Evaluation
- ❑ Narrative

A research paper presents a synthesis of information as a cohesive discussion. You read information, ideas, and perspectives from many different sources. Then you present all of that material in a way that someone else can easily understand. If you wrote an "info dump" and simply gave each piece of information in the order you found it, then your research paper would lack organization, clarity, context, and a sense of purpose. A research paper can be either informative, letting readers make up their own minds, or persuasive, convincing readers to agree with the paper's conclusions or interpretations.

A report is similar to a research paper. Usually, reports focus on gathering together a specific set of data or information. A quarterly report for a business will present data on sales, expenses, logistics, new product development, research and development, and so on. Reports tend to contain many statistics and tables. They may be used or cited in other genres of writing, such as a research paper or an analysis.

An analysis will break down information and explain what it means or why it matters. One might analyze a short story for a literature class, a historical event for sociology, a marketing plan, a production process, or (wait for it) a genre of writing. Analysis often involves some evaluation. You analyze something to reach a conclusion about it — how it works, why it works, whether it is effective or ineffective, how it could be improved, whether it is the best option, and so forth.

Narratives are stories. A good story depends on concrete, sensory details that help readers mentally experience what's being described. An article about the economic struggles of rural communities would do well to describe the hunched shoulders, shuffling steps, and tired eyes of a middle-aged farmer with gray hair and a forehead creased from worry. Your write-up of a customer's testimonial could focus on an employee's smiling, upbeat demeanor.

Sometimes, writers may combine genres in the same piece of writing. A report may include some analysis, or an analysis may be based on research much like a research paper would be. Narratives, in particular, can be useful additions to many other genres. Research papers, reports, or analyses may benefit from adding narratives to illustrate points, contextualize statistics, or put a human face on a topic.

Writing in a Genre

First, find examples of the genre. Then read those examples like a writer.

Next, imitate the genre. Mimic the type of content, the organization, the use of headings (if any), and the style and tone of the writing.

From there, you can begin to make the piece your own if you wish. You shouldn't violate genre conventions or the audience's expectations, but you could add details, narrative, or perspective to make the piece better fit your audience, purpose, and style.

Return to the genre examples, find more examples, or both. Compare what you wrote to the examples. How similar are they? Would someone recognize your piece as belonging to the genre? You may ask for feedback from someone familiar with the genre. If you can't find someone familiar with it, then you could share one of the examples for comparison with your own writing.

Where Does It Fit in the Equation?

Genre helps you determine the audience's expectations, needs, or goals and thus your purpose in communicating to the audience. When writing in a certain genre, knowing that genre's conventions, characteristics, and features reveals what the audience expects, what your purpose is, and how you can fulfill those expectations and achieve that purpose.

If we were to add genre to our equation, we would write:

Audience-awareness + <u>**Purpose**</u> + ...
Genre

To learn and write in a new genre:

- ❏ find examples of the genre;
- ❏ read them like a writer;
- ❏ imitate the genre; and
- ❏ check your writing against the examples.

Here are some thought-exercises and activities to help you understand, analyze, and write within a genre.

Thought-Exercises

1. What are your favorite types of movies or television shows? What characteristics distinguish these movies or shows from others?

2. Do your favorite movies or television shows fit in a certain genre? If so, how would you explain or describe this genre to someone who is unfamiliar with it?

3. Think of the last thing you read. What genre was it? What characteristics distinguished it as this genre?

Activities

1. Write something that imitates your favorite genre of movie or television show.

2. Write something that imitates your favorite or preferred genre to read.

3. Write something that imitates the genre of the last thing you read.

4

Thesis Statements, or the BLUF

A thesis statement is the point, main idea, or central claim of your writing. It conveys the purpose of your writing. The more specific and detailed your thesis, the more clearly it will express your main idea and a sense of purpose.

In chapter two, I advised establishing purpose early, explicitly, and with specific language. An effective thesis statement will come early in your writing. It will explicitly state your main idea, and it will use specific, detailed language to do so.

It can be helpful to think of the thesis statement as the BLUF — the bottom-line, up-front. If you could tell your audience only one idea, the BLUF would be it. It is your main idea, your central claim, and your purpose in communicating.

It is crucial to state your purpose and bottom-line early in the writing so that readers know what to expect, what genre they are reading, and whether it will serve their needs and goals. Assuming they decide it will, a specific and detailed thesis early in your paper helps readers view the rest of your writing as purposeful, focused, and organized.

In most informative or persuasive writing, you will restate your thesis in the conclusion. The first time the audience reads your thesis, they don't necessarily fully understand or agree with it. Hopefully, they will understand and agree with your thesis after reading about each of the specific supporting points and details presented in your paper. Restating your thesis in the conclusion, then, reminds readers of your entire thesis and gives you a chance to present your thesis with maximum impact.

Where's the BLUF?

To illustrate the importance of a strong thesis, or BLUF, here is an example of some writing that lacks a clear thesis (and thus a sense of purpose):

❑ Car technology has progressed so much since the days of the "horseless carriage." Many vehicles have DVD players built-in, Bluetooth connectivity, multiple USB chargers, and even WI-FI. Engines run much better and operate with computers. Drivers do not even use keys any more. They can start their engines, pun intended, with the push of a button, and the doors lock automatically when they walk away from the car with the key. Walking back out to the car to retrieve something but encountering locked doors can be very frustrating.

What is the point, main idea, or central claim of this introductory paragraph? The last sentence of the introduction is usually the thesis statement, but surely the paper won't focus solely on the frustration of encountering locked car doors without a key? There isn't much of a purpose to that idea. It also diverges sharply from most of the rest of the introduction.

The first sentence could be a general thesis. The thesis or BLUF sometimes comes at the very beginning. But the rest of the introduction focuses on modern examples of car technology rather than examples of progress over time. It also ranges over diverse car technology instead of focusing on one type. Is the rest of the paper about car technology? If so, what kind? There are big jumps from built-in DVD players to auto-lock to the frustration of locked doors.

The lack of clarity, focus, and purpose in this introduction demonstrates the importance of a specific, detailed, purposeful thesis statement early in the writing.

Here's the BLUF

In contrast to the example above, the writing below has a clear, specific, detailed, and purposeful thesis statement or BLUF. If this was all you had time to say to your audience, your audience's time would be well-spent.

- ❑ Push-button start, keyless entry, and auto-locking have become widespread vehicle features, causing a fair amount of confusion and inconvenience for households with multiple cars. One person will walk out to the other person's car expecting to open the door and retrieve something, but it will be locked due to the auto-lock feature. Obviously, one can simply carry a key for each vehicle, but then a person with a spouse and multiple driving-age children might have four or five car keys, plus keys for the house and workplace. A new product, The Key Manager, easily syncs with most vehicle models and their keys, allowing drivers to carry one key for multiple cars.

The first few sentences present the problem or situation. The thesis, or BLUF, then sums up the paper's content and purpose with adequate specific detail. Readers know the paper's main idea and purpose, and they will expect a more detailed discussion of The Key Manager and its functions and benefits. When the paper delivers on this promise, it will seem even better developed and organized than it already is. (The Key Manager is hypothetical, by the way.)

Finding Your BLUF

As a writing teacher, I often find myself telling students to work on their thesis statements. Their thesis statements are often too vague, lack a clear purpose, or both.

The problem is not a lack of intelligence or inspiration. The students simply lack strategies for finding their thesis statements, or their BLUFs.

To state a strong thesis, we need to know what we think about a topic. Some people can sit down, think about something, and reach a judgment with several supporting reasons. Then they can write a paper that states their judgment and summarizes its supporting reasons in the very first paragraph. In other words, they write a specific, detailed thesis with a clear purpose.

Other people need help thinking through their ideas. They may use various brainstorming strategies, such as "mind-mapping" or "free-writing." They may thoroughly discuss the topic with someone. They may write an entire draft before really figuring out what they think about the subject of their writing. (For a list of prewriting strategies, refer to chapter 10.)

Whatever kind of person you might be, finding the BLUF takes time and effort.

If you expend that effort up-front by thinking through your draft before starting to write it, then you will probably have a pretty strong thesis in your first draft.

If you need to figure out what you think through the process of drafting, then your first draft will almost certainly lack a decent thesis. You will need to rewrite the draft so that you state a specific, detailed thesis early in your paper, preferably the first paragraph. (For a list of rewriting strategies, refer to chapter 10.)

Rewriting, or revising, strategies can be extremely helpful to discovering your BLUF and how to best express it. These revision strategies include:

❏ underlining the specific details of your thesis;

❑ looking to the conclusion for inspiration; and

❑ reverse-outlining.

When you underline the specific details of your thesis, then you double-check that your thesis actually has specific details. The details are important because they give the thesis its substance and purpose as well as foreshadow the rest of the paper's ideas. If you can't underline anything, then you know you need to add more specific detail that sums up your paper's main points.

Sometimes, I tell students to use their conclusion as the introduction and then write a new conclusion. Their conclusions often have excellent thesis statements because they finally figured out what they thought about the topic. If you look to the conclusion for inspiration, then you can improve your introduction's thesis by adding the details and purpose from your conclusion's thesis. You shouldn't repeat your thesis verbatim, but you want the introduction and conclusion's thesis statements to match up in terms of detail and purpose.

An outline lists the main points you want to make in your essay or speech. Outlines are written before writing a draft, and they are usually written with short phrases that jog a writer or speaker's memory.

Reverse-outlining occurs after writing a draft. Read through your draft and write the main idea of each paragraph in the margin of the paper, in MS Word's "comments," or in separate notes. Limit yourself to short phrases or even individual words if possible. A reverse-outline provides a list of the main points you already made. Then you can write a thesis, or BLUF, in the introduction that sums up those points.

Writing the BLUF

How do you write the thesis, or BLUF, once you find it?

As I will explain more fully in chapter ten, writing is a process. You won't write a perfect draft on the first try, and you likely won't figure out your thesis on the first try either.

Don't worry! There is still "one right answer," or at least a systematic method.

First, understand yourself.

Do you think through things before reaching a conclusion? How much time-to-think do you need? Or do you reach conclusions by talking about things with others? Or writing?

Second, use your strengths.

If you think through your writing before starting a draft, then make sure you take enough time to think and determine your thesis before beginning to write. You may go through multiple drafts of your thesis, or BLUF, in your mind.

If you need to have some discussions with others or do some prewriting or drafting to determine what you think on a topic, then remember that you will need to revise your introduction's thesis statement more thoroughly than someone who revised it mentally before writing it down. Remember that your first draft is tentative and that its purpose is to get you to a better final draft.

Third, use revision strategies as needed.

You may thoroughly contemplate and mentally revise a thesis statement, but you could still benefit from underlining its specific details, checking the conclusion's thesis, or reverse-outlining. One of these strategies may be more helpful to you than the others, or you may find different ones to be helpful at different times.

Fourth, practice audience-awareness. Put yourself in the reader's shoes. Ask yourself, "Will my audience know what this paper covers? Will they know what to expect from the rest of the paper?" You may show your thesis — and only your thesis — to a friend and then ask these questions.

Whatever you do, always ensure that your thesis contains specific details that foreshadow the paper's main ideas and express a sense of purpose.

Where Does It Fit in the Equation?

Your audience should know what your writing covers and why it matters, based solely on your thesis or BLUF statement. Readers are always wondering:

- ❏ So what?
- ❏ Why should I care?
- ❏ What will I get out of this?
- ❏ Will this meet my needs, achieve my goals, or enable an action I want to take?

A specific, detailed, purposeful thesis statement answers each of these questions. The more specific and detailed it is, the more substantive it will be. The more substantive, the more it will establish purpose and engage interest.

We can add to the equation:

Audience-Awareness + <u>Purpose</u> + Thesis + …
Genre

As you can see, audience-awareness, purpose, genre, and thesis are all interrelated. You are well on your way to learning how to write an essay like an equation.

Here are some thought-exercises and activities to develop your thesis statement and BLUF-ing skills (sorry, not sorry).

Thought-Exercises

1. Think about the last time you were really confused by someone or something, such as a conversation, a video, or a piece of writing. Why was it hard to figure out the main idea and follow along?

2. Think about the last time you struggled to explain yourself. If you could re-explain, what would you say now?

3. How would you sum up the last article or book you read (or movie you watched) in less than thirty words?

Activities

1. Write a summary, in thirty words or less, of the last article or book that you read. Include as many main ideas as you can.

2. Choose an article or book. Write the main idea or central claim in your own words. Be specific.

3. Think about a hobby or subject that you enjoy. In thirty words or less, tell someone unfamiliar with the hobby or subject both what it is and why you enjoy it.

5

PEE Paragraph Structure

Once you have written the thesis statement, or BLUF, you must develop and support it with more detail. The BLUF might be the essential information that your audience must know, but if the BLUF were sufficient by itself, then you wouldn't be asked to write a whole paper about it.

Why? To fully understand your thesis or BLUF, the reader needs the details, examples, and explanations that you know and which helped you write the thesis or BLUF in the first place. The thesis statement establishes your writing's purpose, presents your main idea, and outlines and foreshadows the rest of your paper's ideas. The rest of the paper develops those ideas so that the reader can fully understand, and agree with, your thesis statement. This is how you simultaneously serve the audience's needs and achieve your purpose in communicating.

As a writing teacher, I see many papers that struggle to support their thesis statements. Often, these papers don't connect the information in their paragraphs back to the thesis in the introduction. It's not clear how the information relates to or supports the paper's main idea.

There may be a lot of information, but it reads like an "info dump" in which the writer dumped information into the paper for no particular purpose and in no particular order, leaving the reader to figure out the purpose and organization.

Or the paragraphs relate back to the thesis, but the information itself doesn't adequately support the ideas stated in the thesis.

PEE Paragraph Structure is an effective, flexible technique for ensuring that your paragraphs support your thesis. It provides a structure for relating information back to your thesis and checking that you have provided adequate supporting information in the first place.

What is PEE?

PEE stands for "point-evidence-explanation." Every paragraph should have a clear point sentence at or near the beginning. Then the paragraph should present evidence that explains and supports the point. Lastly, the paragraph should explain the evidence and how it supports the paragraph's point and the paper's thesis.

Point Sentences

A point sentence is the same thing as a topic sentence. Whatever you call them, the first sentence (or two) of a paragraph should tell the reader what the paragraph is about.

I prefer the term "point sentence" over the more common term "topic sentence" because it emphasizes the idea of purpose. A paragraph with a topic sentence may or may not relate to the purpose of the writing. A well-written point sentence will be purposeful.

Let's say that your boss asked you to evaluate different health insurance options for a small business and then write an email sharing your evaluation. After careful research, you decide that the best option would be to buy into a group insurance plan.

You could begin a paragraph in that email with the sentence, "Employees should be encouraged to eat avocados since they are very nutritious." Then you could provide evidence about avocados' healthfulness. There is a topic sentence, but what purpose does the topic serve in helping the email achieve its purpose?

In that same email, you might begin a paragraph, "There are twenty-seven other small businesses in our area that may be interested in banding together to buy into a group insurance plan." That paragraph has a topic, but more importantly, it has a point.

The point sentence announces what the paragraph is about, but that's not all it does. It also makes a point that relates back to the thesis (in this case, "Buying into a group insurance plan is the best option"). It has a specific purpose that supports the writing's overall purpose.

Make sure each paragraph you write has a clear point sentence, an announcement of a purposeful topic. The point sentence should clearly relate to some specific detail from your thesis or BLUF.

Evidence

After writing your point sentence, provide evidence that backs up the point. There are three categories of evidence:

- ❑ logical appeals;
- ❑ emotional appeals; and
- ❑ appeals based on credibility.

There are dozens of specific kinds of evidence within each category. Rather than drown you in details, let's take a big picture view.

First, evidence should be relevant, legitimate, and based on sound reasoning.

Second, emotional appeals should enhance logical appeals, not substitute for, or distract from, a lack of logic.

Third, make authentic appeals to credibility.

Fourth, understand and appeal to the audience's values, beliefs, and attitudes.

Let's say you are writing a persuasive essay arguing that climate change results from a natural process rather than human activity, namely burning fossil fuels. You could construct a logical argument that the earth's climate has changed over periods of time long before humans started burning fossil fuels in mass quantities.

However, this argument would be irrelevant, illegitimate, and based on faulty reasoning. The issue is not climate change but how rapidly it is changing. It is irrelevant to today's climate change that earth's climate changed in the past. There also isn't any legitimate scientific evidence that CO_2 doesn't cause a greenhouse effect. Therefore, the logic of a natural process versus man-made climate change doesn't hold up when you contextualize the speed of our current warming trend compared to past evolutions in climate.

When you use emotional appeals, they should enhance the logical evidence rather than substitute for them. You can argue against burning fossil fuels with emotional stories of climate change's worst effects on communities, as long as your descriptions remain scientifically accurate and enhance other forms of evidence. You wouldn't want to rely entirely on emotional appeals because by themselves they wouldn't prove that CO2 emissions cause climate change.

Make authentic appeals to credibility. Don't portray yourself as an expert if you're not. Don't claim experience you don't have. If you lack expertise or experience, then do some research, cite that research, and allow the expertise and experience of others to build your own credibility.

Grounding evidence in the audience's values is crucial to all types of appeals. You don't pander, but you meet the audience where they are and lessen the mental distance the audience has to travel to be persuaded.

For instance, if you want to persuade business leaders to support raising taxes to build a new dam, then you should demonstrate that the dam would yield enough benefits to businesses to make the taxes worth it. You would provide research and give examples showing that the dam will control flooding, prevent disasters, and lower insurance costs.

If you were arguing for building a dam to conservationists, then those same appeals wouldn't be as persuasive. Conservationists have different values than business leaders, generally speaking. So instead, you would want to share examples of similar dams preserving habitat for local species and creating new areas for hiking, camping, and fishing.

You don't make up evidence to fit the audience. You select the existing evidence that will be most relevant and persuasive to the intended audience.

Explanation

After providing evidence, you should explain the evidence to your audience. You may need to explain what the evidence says if it is complex or difficult to understand. Whether it is very confusing or very simple, you will need to explain exactly how the evidence supports your main idea, central claim, or thesis.

I see many student papers that fall short in their explanation. They assume the evidence speaks for itself, but this is rarely the case.

If you argue against mandatory vaccinations, your thesis might focus on religious exceptions: "Vaccinations should not be required for people with religious objections."

A point sentence could be, "Allowing people with religious objections to remain unvaccinated will not pose a significant risk to public health." (This isn't actually true. One large religious population in New York City has gone unvaccinated and has been stricken with many measles cases. But go with me for a moment.)

The evidence could be a statement like, "Herd immunity will prevent contagious diseases from popping up among the small number of people who would not be vaccinated."

Imagine if we left it at that? Would the connections among the thesis, point sentence, and evidence be clear to the reader?

If the intended audience were medical professionals, then the evidence might speak for itself. But for most readers, you would need to explain the evidence so that it clearly connects back to the point it tries to prove and the thesis it tried to support.

The explanation would be, "Since everyone else in the population will be vaccinated, there will not be any prevalence of contagious illnesses like measles or polio. Absent such prevalence, the unvaccinated will be safe from disease as if they had been vaccinated."

Now there is a clear connection among the thesis, point sentence, and evidence. The reader doesn't have to guess how the evidence relates to the thesis.

Let's look at one more example. You've been asked to explain the process of ocean acidification. Your thesis is, "Oceans absorb CO2, which makes the water's pH acidic."

One of your point sentences says, "Data confirms a more acidic pH in saltwater with higher CO2 levels."

You present the evidence, "One scientific study measured pH and CO2 levels in a sample of the Atlantic Ocean. Then the researchers took another sample, removed some CO2, and measured the pH. It was much less acidic than the first sample."

Resist the temptation to think the evidence speaks for itself. Readers don't want to think more than necessary, so don't make them decide what they think about the evidence. Tell them what it means and what to think about it relative to your thesis.

For example, "The results of this study indicate a causal link between rising CO2 levels and ocean acidification."

Without the explanation, the reader would have to connect the evidence back to the thesis. With the explanation, you make the connection crystal clear for the reader.

Where's the PEE?

To illustrate PEE structure's effectiveness, here is an example paragraph that lacks this technique:

> ❑ Many people are deeply religious. Because of herd immunity, they should not be required to receive vaccinations. Babies today are given so many shots in their first two years. Schools require vaccinations for students. Doctors say everyone needs vaccines. We must respect religion.

How does the point sentence about religiosity relate to vaccinations? What is herd immunity? Why does it matter to vaccinations?

Here's another example:

> ❑ CO2 emissions have been increasing since the dawn of the Industrial Revolution. The pH of ocean water can change in response to pollution. Chemical processes bind CO2 to H2O and then pH changes. Ocean acidification is a major part of climate change.

There are four point sentences here, each lacking context, evidence, or explanation.

There's the PEE

Here are some examples of effective PEE structure. They are the same as the earlier examples, but I think it's helpful to see the sentences together:

- ❏ Allowing people with religious objections to remain unvaccinated will not pose a significant risk to public health. Herd immunity will prevent contagious diseases from popping up among the small number of people who would not be vaccinated. Since everyone else in the population will be vaccinated, there will not be any prevalence of contagious illnesses like measles or polio. Absent such prevalence, the unvaccinated will be safe from disease as if they had been vaccinated.

- ❏ Data confirms a more acidic pH in saltwater with higher CO_2 levels. One scientific study measured pH and CO_2 levels in a sample of the Atlantic Ocean. Then the researchers took another sample, removed some CO_2, and measured the pH. It was much less acidic than the first sample. The results of this study indicate a causal link between rising CO_2 levels and ocean acidification.

Each of these example paragraphs offers a clear point, supporting evidence, and explanation of the evidence.

(Again, allowing significant populations to remain unvaccinated has posed a public health risk time and again; it's important to recognize how PEE can help develop a decent argument for bad ideas, both to illustrate PEE's effectiveness and to help us be on guard.)

Even in a shorter, less formal piece of writing, PEE can be helpful. Consider the Customer Appreciation Party flyer.

> ❏ You're invited! Stress-Free Tax Prep will host a Customer Appreciation Party at its main office, May 1st at 12:00 pm, to thank you for your business and celebrate another stress-free tax season. Join us for BBQ, drinks, door prizes, and fun games for the family.

The point sentence gets the main idea across in a purposeful way: "You're invited!" The evidence provides the information needed to attend and the motivation behind the party. The explanation makes the case for attending.

Breaking Up Paragraphs

A large block of uninterrupted text can intimidate readers before they even begin reading. Moreover, each paragraph should develop one main point.

So avoid excessively long paragraphs. Any paragraph more than half a page in length can be broken up at some point. Look for a place where one main point ends and a new main point begins. The new main point may be a "sub-point," but it can still warrant its own paragraph.

In certain genres of books, articles, or reports, you could get away with longer paragraphs, but that doesn't mean you should. In some genres or media, a paragraph should be far shorter than half a page. Pay attention to paragraph length when you read and learn a new genre. Use your judgement for when a paragraph looks overwhelming for the genre or medium.

For example, I could have written the previous two paragraphs as one larger paragraph. They both focus on the main idea of paragraph length. But I basically wrapped up one point with "The new point may …" and started a new, distinct subpoint with "In certain genres …." If I were writing a physical book or a scholarly article, I probably would have left the paragraphs combined. Since I'm writing an e-book, I broke them up.

Where Does It Fit in the Equation?

Using PEE Structure, you can develop and organize content in a systematic fashion. It helps   connect the information in your paragraphs back to your thesis, creating a focused, unified piece of writing. The point sentence relates to the thesis, the evidence supports the point (and thus the thesis), and the explanation tells readers how the evidence supports the point (and thesis). PEE structure helps ensure that each sentence contributes to meeting your audience's needs and achieving your purpose in communicating.

PEE Structure multiplies Thesis (and vice-versa) in our equation:

Audience-Awareness + <u>Purpose</u> + Thesis(PEE) + ...
Genre

Here are some thought-exercises and activities to improve your paragraph development and organization.

Thought-Exercises

1. Think about the last time that you found a conversation or written paragraph confusing and hard to follow. Could PEE have made it clearer? How so?

2. Think about the last time you really understood a conversation or paragraph. How did PEE help develop and structure the ideas?

3. How do most news articles subtly use PEE?

Activities

1. Pick a paragraph at random from an article or book. Identify its point, evidence, and explanation.

2. Does the evidence convince you of the point? Why or why not?

3. Does the explanation help convince you? Or connect the point to the main idea or thesis? Why or why not?

4. Write a PEE paragraph on a hobby or subject that you enjoy.

6

Content-Lexical Ties

In earlier chapters, we learned about three essential concepts for knowing how to approach a writing task: audience, purpose, and genre. Then we learned techniques for developing and organizing written content: clear, specific, detailed thesis statements (or BLUFs) backed up with paragraphs structured according to point-evidence-explanation.

Now, we turn to techniques for enhancing the organization of your writing and achieving the mysterious "flow" that writing teachers talk about. You may have been told that your writing doesn't flow well, but were you taught what that meant? More importantly, were you told how to fix it? Or perhaps you have been told that your writing flows well. Do you understand how or why?

Learning about content-lexical ties will help you understand and accomplish the "flow" that takes writing up a notch or two. The more your writing "flows," the easier readers comprehend it. The more easily they comprehend it, the more easily they accept your ideas and the more highly they will rate your writing.

What is "Flow" Anyway?

When we talk about "flow," we are talking about cohesion. Cohesion means unity or "sticking together." When two things are cohesive, they stick together into one whole.

Cohesion in language, either spoken or written, refers to the unity or "sticking together" of ideas due to how they are expressed.

How do we express ideas so that they stick together or "flow"? We use content-lexical ties.

What are Content-Lexical Ties?

Let's break down the term. Content, of course, refers to the ideas or information we present. Lexical is the adjective form of lexicon, which is a fancy word for vocabulary. A vocabulary is simply a storehouse of words. When you see "lexical," think "words." A tie binds things together.

Content-lexical ties are words (lexicon) that tie (bind) different pieces of content (ideas) together into a cohesive whole. To put it another way, writing that "flows" uses certain types of words to connect new ideas to earlier ideas.

The Four Types of Content-Lexical Ties

There are four types of content-lexical ties (adapted from linguist Dilin Liu).

Table 1. Types of Content-Lexical Ties (Adapted from Liu)			
Direct Repetition, Synonyms, Antonyms	Related Words (Contextual Synonyms or Antonyms)	Categories and Members of Categories	Transition Sentences, Phrases, or Words

Type 1: Direct Repetition, Synonyms, and Antonyms

The first type of content-lexical tie consists of directly repeating key words and using synonyms, antonyms, or both to restate ideas without repeating the same words too much. Repeating key words at strategic places in your writing will simultaneously emphasize and connect ideas, facilitating comprehension and maintaining interest.

Too much repetition, however, will become mind-numbing. Using synonyms allows you to restate key ideas without using the same exact words. Antonyms create contrasts with earlier ideas or wording, connecting that previous content with the current passage in your writing.

Notice how I used repetition, synonyms, and antonyms to connect ideas and create a smooth "flow" in the paragraph above? Let's take a closer look. Below, the bold words are repetitions, and the bold-and-italic words are synonyms or antonyms.

❑ The first type of content-lexical tie consists of directly **repeating key words** and using **synonyms, antonyms**, or both to *restate ideas* without **repeating** the **same words**. **Repeating key words** at strategic places in **your writing** will simultaneously emphasize and connect **ideas**, facilitating comprehension and maintaining *interest*. Too much **repetition**, however, will become *mind-numbing*. Using **synonyms** allows you to *restate key ideas* without using the same exact words. **Antonyms** create contrasts with earlier **ideas** or *wording*, connecting that previous *content* with the current *passage* in **your writing**.

The direct repetition, such as "repeating key words" in the first and second sentences, connects the information in those sentences to each other. Using synonyms, such as "restate ideas" and "repetition" for "repeating key words," also connects ideas but without excessive repetition. Similarly, "wording," "ideas," "passage," and "writing" function as synonyms. The words "interest" and "mind-numbing" are antonyms. A contrasting relationship between one idea and another connects those ideas as well as the ideas around them.

Type 2: Related Words

So-called "related words" are the second type of content-lexical tie. Related words are contextual synonyms or antonyms. A "related word" wouldn't normally mean the same thing or the opposite as another word, but it becomes a synonym or antonym in the context in which it is used.

Relying entirely on repetition and restatement can easily lead to stale writing. It's very helpful to use related words to maintain variety while connecting ideas across a piece of writing. The words "flow" and "cohesion" don't have the same dictionary definitions, but they mean the same thing in the context of writing. "Disorganized" and "flow" don't mean the opposite of each other except when talking about writing. "Stale" and "variety" aren't antonyms, but they become antonyms in the context of this paragraph. The previous sentence relates to the previous paragraph: "it [a related word] becomes a synonym or antonym in the context in which it is used."

Related words are so effective because they are hardly noticed. They make the reading experience very smooth, but they don't call attention to themselves as much as the other types of content-lexical ties. Thus, they create subtle but strong cohesion throughout a piece of writing.

Type 3: Categories and Members of Categories

Categories and members of those categories comprise the third type of content-lexical tie.

This book, section, and paragraph are organized with categories and members thereof. The book is about writing, and each chapter explains a strategy or component of writing. In this section, I stated that there are four types of content-lexical ties, and then I named and explained each type. This paragraph begins with "book, section, and paragraph" and then discusses each one in turn. Implicitly, they are members of the category of writing. More explicitly, "section" and "paragraph" are members of "book." Stating categories and their members can help structure writing on the levels of entire books and single paragraphs, achieving flow and cohesion.

Sometimes the subject matter lends itself to using categories and members, and sometimes it does not. Don't force categories or members into your writing if they don't fit. Having said that, if you expand your thinking about them, then you may identify more kinds of categories than you would expect. As shown above, depending on context, "writing" can be a category and "book, section, and paragraph" can be members of that category.

Type 4: Transition Sentences, Phrases, and Words

Each of the content-lexical ties above creates implicit, or indirectly suggested, connections among ideas. In contrast, transitions explicitly, or directly, tell readers how one idea relates to another. They usually occur at the beginning of paragraphs or sentences so that they help readers interpret the writing as they read it.

The transition word "therefore" tells readers that the next idea results from the previous one. The same is true for transition phrases like "as a result" or "in consequence."

The transition word "however" tells readers that the next idea in some way contradicts the previous one. So do transition phrases such as "to the contrary" or "in contrast."

Phrases like "for example" signal that the next idea elaborates on a prior one, while a phrase such as "since then" indicates a relationship of time.

You must use the transition word or phrase that signals the relationship that you want to convey. Here is a list of common transition words and phrases, organized according to their meanings:

Table 2. Common Transitions Grouped by their Meanings		
Cause-Effect/ Conclusion	**Addition/ Elaboration**	**Comparison**
Accordingly,	Also,	Also,
As a result,	Furthermore,	Similarly,
Consequently,	Moreover,	Likewise,
Hence,	In addition,	Equally,
It follows ...	Additionally,	In the same way,
Since	Indeed,	In comparison,
Thus,	In fact,	Comparatively,
Therefore,	In other words,	Just like[A], B is ...
Ultimately,	To put it another way,	Along the same lines,
Conclusion	**Concession**	**Example**
In short,	Admittedly	For example,
In brief,	Granted	For instance,
To summarize,	I concede ...	As an example,
To sum up,	While it is true ...	As an illustration
Lastly,	Even though ...	Specifically,
Finally,	Although it is true ...	Another example is ...
Contrast	**Time/Order**	
However,	First [Second, etc.],	
On the contrary,	Last,	
On the other hand,	Next,	
Conversely,	Then	
Regardless,	Beforehand,	
Whereas	Afterward,	
While		
Although		
Even though		

Using appropriate transition words and phrases easily but effectively improves your writing's flow. Add them to the beginning of paragraphs or sentences that start a new topic, point, or idea. Add them to sentences that need a stronger connection to earlier ideas in the writing. Directly stating relationships between ideas builds bridges that facilitate comprehension and create cohesion.

By stating the relationship between one paragraph and the next, transition sentences guide readers between the paragraphs. An effective transition sentence communicates two things: the main idea of the previous paragraph and the main idea, or point, of the paragraph into which you are transitioning. It is even more effective when you state the idea of the previous paragraph's last sentence and then the point of the upcoming paragraph. This technique creates a strong bridge between the paragraphs.

In the paragraph above, for example, the first sentence refers back to the prior paragraph's last sentence — "By stating the relationship between one paragraph and the next" refers to "Directly stating relationships between ideas." The rest of the sentence states the upcoming topic, transition sentences.

Transition sentences often use phrases like, "In addition to ...," or "In contrast to ...," or "Although ...," or "Similar to ...," to set up both the reference to a prior idea and the statement of the next idea.

There are many more such phrases you might use, but I find these phrases to be quite flexible.

- ❏ "In addition to directly stating relationships among ideas, transitions add length to writing without being fluff."
- ❏ "In contrast to directly stating relationships among ideas, other content-lexical ties imply the relationships."
- ❏ "Although stating relationships between ideas is important, it cannot substitute for strong audience-awareness, purpose, and development of ideas."
- ❏ "Similar to directly stating relationships among ideas, implying or suggesting connections also guides readers."

Notice that you can connect an idea or sentence to the next one in a variety of ways, depending on the nature of the idea into which you are transitioning. Use the phrasing that helps set up the kind of statement you want to make.

Whenever you need to improve the flow from one paragraph to the next, try the simple technique of writing a sentence that refers back to the previous paragraph or sentence and then states the main idea or point of the upcoming paragraph.

Combining Content-Lexical Ties

Ideally, you will use each type of content-lexical tie in the same piece of writing. Combining them will give you more flexibility in connecting your ideas for the reader. You don't necessarily have to make sure you work in an antonym for the sake of doing so, especially if doing so would be awkward, but it should be fairly easy to find opportunities to incorporate some of each type.

Here is an example of a paragraph that combines all four types to create cohesion through both implicit and explicit connections among the ideas:

❑ Renewable energy sources include solar, wind, and geothermal power. Solar power comes from solar panels, which are usually located in very sunny climates like deserts. The panels convert energy from the sun into electricity that can be transported or stored. Wind power comes from huge wind turbines located in open plains where strong winds blow almost incessantly. These turbines connect to generators, turning them to produce electricity. Lastly, geothermal power uses heat from underground sources to produce steam used by electric plants. While they hold promise, these sources can de-energize electric plants and disempower homes when clouds fill the sky, the wind stops, or the underground heat lessens.

Type 1: Words like "energy," "solar," and "power" are repeated throughout. "Energy" and "electricity" are synonyms. "Energy" and "de-energize" are antonyms.

Type 2: The word "power" is a contextual synonym, or related word, for "energy" and "electricity." The word "disempower" is a contextual antonym.

Type 3: The passage begins with a category, "renewable energy sources," and then describes members of that category, "solar, wind, and geothermal power."

Type 4: The word "lastly" guides readers from the previous sentence into the upcoming sentence. The phrase, "while they hold promise," similarly guides readers into the concluding sentence's idea.

With just a little thoughtfulness, you can create numerous connections among your ideas, facilitate comprehension, and provide a smooth reading experience.

How to Use Content-Lexical Ties

There are two ways to apply content-lexical ties to your writing. Don't worry. Pick the answer that is right for you. Try both if you're not sure. They're pretty similar anyway.

Option 1: you can consciously incorporate content-lexical ties as you write. You could write a point sentence and begin your supporting evidence. Then you could ask yourself, "How can I connect what I'm going to write back to those earlier ideas?"

That general question may suffice, but it should also help with asking and answering more specific questions:

- ❏ What key words or ideas should I repeat strategically?
- ❏ What synonyms or antonyms can I use to restate key ideas?
- ❏ In this context, what words or phrases would be related to each other and/or to what I have already written?
- ❏ Have I discussed any categories? Should I? If so, what members of those categories should I mention now?
- ❏ Would a transition sentence bridge between two ideas or sentences?
- ❏ Would a transition word or phrase guide the reader into an idea, topic, or sentence?

Option 2: you can incorporate content-lexical ties while rewriting and editing. Write the draft of your paragraph or entire paper. Read it and look for the content-lexical ties that you used (or didn't). Then add more of them as needed.

Where Does It Fit in the Equation?

By making both implicit and explicit connections among ideas, content-lexical ties create cohesion within any length of writing. Readers experience this cohesion as a smooth "flow" from idea to the next.

Content-lexical ties, or CLTs for short, enhance the existing development, organization, and structure of a piece of writing. So we would add it to our equation like so:

Audience-Awareness + **<u>Purpose</u>** + Thesis(PEE) + CLTs + ...
Genre

Here are some thought-exercises and activities to help you use content-lexical ties.

Thought-Exercises

1. Now that you know what they are, consider how content-lexical ties help a conversation or piece of writing "flow" for you.

2. Think about how you might restate an idea several times without seeming to repeat yourself.

3. How many ways can you transition between a sentence about "kumquats" and a sentence about "machinery"?

Activities

1. Pick a paragraph or two out of an article at random. Identify the content-lexical ties.

2. Rewrite the same paragraph in your own words, coming up with your own content-lexical ties.

3. Write a paragraph in which you use all four types of content-lexical ties.

7

The Paramedic Method of Editing

Writing should be clear, concise, and precise. A strong writing style allows your voice to come through to readers, engaging their interest. It also respects the reader's time and attention by not wasting either.

Unfortunately, schools create bad writing habits such as habitually vague, wordy, convoluted sentences. Teachers ask students to write ten pages on a topic without equipping or motivating them to do so. Predictably, students write a lot of "fluff" and pad their sentences. Sometimes they even earn A grades. Then they enter the workforce, and their bosses, coworkers, and clients bemoan their poor writing.

Fortunately, this chapter has a solution. It will either prevent you from developing bad writing habits to begin with or exorcise those habits from your writing. It revolutionized my writing, and I'm excited to share it with you!

Examples of Wordy Writing

But first, I want to emphasize the problems of bad writing habits since they can be surprisingly difficult to spot. We become used to seeing such writing, and then we stop seeing it. Here is the first example:

- ❑ But the sad reality is that there are people out there that rely on the virtual world rather than their own.

This sounds good, doesn't it? But let's break it down:

- ❑ But the sad reality is
- ❑ that there are people out there
- ❑ that rely
- ❑ on the virtual world
- ❑ rather than their own.

See how choppy it is? Read it out loud, and you'll notice the sentence's unnecessary repetition as well as its awkwardness: "the sad reality is that there are people out there that rely on the virtual world rather than their own." What's the action? Who's doing it?

Let me be clear. Personal preference is not why I advocate concise writing.

When writing is wordy and imprecise, then readers must work harder to figure out what it means. When readers work harder, they blame the writer for not doing a good job. And they're correct. Wordy writers fail to communicate as effectively as they could.

Here's another example of wordy, convoluted writing that obscures meaning:

❑ Although the War on Drugs has seized considerable amounts of narcotics and convictions, it can be seen that it is an ineffective strategy in the deterrence of crime as a result of its contributing to an increase in corruption and immense government spending despite narcotics still flooding the streets of the United States.

Again, this sounds like the kind of intelligent, developed writing that deserves an A grade. But break it down, and you will see how much meaningless "dead weight" the sentence contains:

❏ Although the War on Drugs has seized considerable amounts

❏ of narcotics and convictions, it can be seen

❏ that it is an ineffective strategy

❏ in the deterrence

❏ of crime as a result

❏ of its contributing

❏ to an increase

❏ in corruption and immense government spending

❏ despite narcotics still flooding the streets

❏ of the United States.

There are so many prepositional phrases (phrases that begin with a preposition like "in" or "of" or "to") that the sentence reads as very choppy. There are unnecessary verb phrases like "it can be seen that it is …." Readers have more difficulty understanding sentences when they must sort through their parts to determine what is meaningful or important and what is not.

Both of these example sentences use many words to communicate very little actual content. They make readers work harder, and they obscure both meaning and the writer's "voice."

What is the Paramedic Method of Editing?

Richard Lanham developed what he calls the "paramedic method of editing" to transform convoluted sentences into clear, crisp writing. It is a systematic approach to editing sentence structure. Once you internalize its principles, you will write better sentences from the start and won't need to edit as much.

Here are the steps of the paramedic method (slightly adapted from Lanham):

- ❏ find a long, wordy sentence;
- ❏ circle the "to be" verbs: am, is, are, was, were, will be, had been, have been, would be, or would have been;
- ❏ draw a line before each preposition (words like "of," "at," "from," "to," etc.);
- ❏ Or if you edit an electronic file, make the "to be" verbs bold and hit "enter" before each preposition to start a new line or paragraph;
- ❏ identify the action in the sentence;
- ❏ state the action in a strong "action verb" that creates an image in your mind, like "push" or "pull" or "punch;"
- ❏ identify the actor doing the action;
- ❏ state the actor and action early in the sentence;
- ❏ delete as much of the sentence as you can, especially the prepositional phrases; and

❑ read the edited sentence out loud to check its content and flow.

Let's apply these steps to the examples above:

❑ But the sad reality is

❑ that there are people out there

❑ that rely

❑ on the virtual world

❑ rather than their own.

We have done the first three steps of the paramedic method: locate a wordy sentence; highlight the "to be" verbs like "is" and "are;" and break up the sentence before each prepositional phrase like "that there …" and "on the …;"

Now, what is the action? What "action verb" would express it in a vivid way? Who is doing the action?

In this sentence, the action is "rely." Rely is a fairly strong action verb. It possesses clear meaning, whereas "to be" verbs are vague in meaning.

Who is doing the action? Who is relying? "People."

State the actor and action early in the sentence. "People rely …."

Delete as much of the sentence as you can, especially the prepositional phrases. Do we need "But the sad reality is" when we state the actor and action early ("People rely")? No.

Do we need "that there are people out there that rely" when we are beginning with "People rely"? No.

Do we need "on the virtual world"? Yes. That phrase tells readers what people rely on.

Do we need "rather than their own"? No. If people rely "on the virtual world," then of course they are not relying "on their own."

So, we are left with:

- ❑ "People rely on the virtual world."
- ❑ Or if you prefer, "Sadly, many people rely on the virtual world."

To check the sentence, read it out loud. Make sure you did not lose any significant or important information. Ensure that the edited sentence reads or flows smoothly.

If we were cutting the sentence down to the bone, then the first edited version would work best. If we wanted a transition, "Sadly," would work well. If we wanted to hedge our claim and not overgeneralize, then adding "many" before "people" would serve that purpose.

Either way, the idea of the sentence becomes dramatically clearer, the writing becomes much more efficient, and both edited sentences have much greater impact on the reader.

Let's tackle the next example:

- ❑ Although the War on Drugs has seized considerable amounts
- ❑ of narcotics and convictions, it can be seen
- ❑ that it is an ineffective strategy
- ❑ in the deterrence
- ❑ of crime as a result
- ❑ of its contributing
- ❑ to an increase
- ❑ in corruption and immense government spending
- ❑ despite narcotics still flooding the streets
- ❑ of the United States.

The sentence has been identified as wordy and convoluted in its structure. The "to be" verbs have been highlighted, and the sentence has been broken down according to its prepositional phrases.

What is the action? The action is "deterrence." Except "deterrence" is a noun, not a verb. The sentence's action hides in plain sight as a noun. To bring it out of hiding, let's use "deter."

Who is the actor? There are many nouns and thus many potential subjects, but look carefully. What deters? "The War on Drugs."

Except "the War on Drugs … is an ineffective strategy in the deterrence …." So the actor is not deterring.

Let's state the actor and action early in the sentence: "The War on Drugs does not deter."

Now delete as much meaningless "dead weight" from the sentence as possible.

Do we need "Although the War on Drugs has seized considerable amounts of narcotics and conventions"? No, not if the sentence's focus lies with deterring instead of seizing.

Do we need "it can be seen"? No. You can delete that phrase or idea without losing the meaning and focus of the sentence, "The War on Drugs does not deter."

Do we need "it is an ineffective strategy in the deterrence of crime"? No. If it doesn't deter crime, then it is ineffective. The idea that it doesn't deter crime includes (by implication) the idea of ineffectiveness.

What about "as a result of …" and the subsequent list of supporting reasons? Yes and no. Yes, the information helps explain why "The War on Drugs does not deter crime." But no, the information is not essential to the statement.

So, we might be left with:

- ❏ "The War on Drugs does not deter crime."
- ❏ Or "The War on Drugs does not deter crime and increases government corruption and spending."

The first edited sentence focuses on the core point. It works best if we are cutting sentences down to the bone or simply focusing the paragraph on only one key point.

The second edited sentence adds some of the supporting reasons. If we were writing a thesis or BLUF, then the second sentence would have superior specificity and detail. It would also work better if we wanted to introduce more ideas to discuss in the paragraph or in later paragraphs.

Either way, the edited sentence achieves far more clarity and thus impact. It also frees up much more room to develop the other ideas in more detail. The writer has many more words in which to discuss crime, corruption, and government spending.

Applying the Paramedic Method of Editing

To apply the paramedic method of editing to your own writing, read through your draft and identify the wordy, convoluted sentences that have meaningless "dead weight." Then go through each of the method's steps.

Student readers will say, "Wait a minute! I need to write a five-page paper. I need more words, not fewer." I understand the concern about filling pages and the temptation to write in a wordy style. Resist the temptation!

You can have the best of both worlds. Write in the clear, concise style of the paramedic method, and then add lists of details and information.

For example, "Sadly, many people rely on the virtual world, such as email, texting, Facebook, Twitter, SnapChat, YouTube, online gaming, mobile gaming, and Massive Multiplayer Online Role Playing Games (MMORGs) like World of Warcraft."

The sentence's point comes across clearly. The list of supporting examples or details also comes across clearly, and it adds significant length without being "fluff" or wordy.

For another example, "The War on Drugs does not deter crime, including nonviolent offenses such as theft or burglary and violent offenses like armed robbery or gang shootings."

Or what about, "The War on Drugs increases government corruption, ranging from officers taking bribes from gangs and drug cartels to government contractors inflating the prices of their contract bids."

Or still yet, one could write, "The War on Drugs increases government spending on federal law enforcement, grants for local police and sheriffs, border security at ports-of-entry, coast guard patrols, the Drug Enforcement Administration, the court system, and prisons."

In each of these sentences, the point and the details come across clearly without being bogged down in "fluff" or awkward structures like "It can be seen that there is corruption that is a problem that it is up to the government to find a solution to."

While you might think "fluff" will help, I assure you of three outcomes if you embrace the paramedic method style of writing.

First, readers (including teachers who grade your work) will greatly appreciate a clear, concise, precise style of writing in which every word offers meaning, and thus reward, for the effort of reading it.

Second, it will be much easier to fill pages when you give yourself many details to expand upon as opposed to figuring out how to pack "fluff" throughout several pages without losing your sanity. It's harder to write sentences like "the problem is that there is an issue that is difficult that is in need of resolution" than "the difficult issue needs a solution, such as …."

In each of the good examples above, you could write a paragraph on each specific detail provided. Your brainstorming would be done for you simply by trying to provide substantive information rather than "fluff."

And third, you will be far better prepared for writing outside the classroom. Outside the classroom, the problem is seldom, "How do I fill so many pages with what I have to say?" but is much more often, "How do I fit what I need to say into so few pages?"

If you can convey an idea in ten words instead of thirty, then you will make a greater impact on your reader, respect the reader's time, and create much more space in which to communicate.

Where Does It Fit in the Equation?

Audience-awareness, purpose, and genre help writers to identify and fulfill the audience's expectations, needs, or goals. A strong thesis statement supported by well-developed point-evidence-explanation (PEE) paragraphs provides the content that the audience needs. Content-lexical ties (CLTs) enhance the PEE development, organization, and structure. The paramedic method ensures clear expression of the content and allows CLTs to shine through instead of being lost amid meaningless "dead weight." Using the paramedic method respects readers' time and more effectively meets their needs or enables their action.

We then add the paramedic method to the end of the equation:

Audience-Awareness +   Purpose + Thesis(PEE) + CLTs + PM +
….

Genre

Here are some thought-exercises and activities to build your awareness of "wordy" writing, your concision, and your writing voice.

Thought-Exercises

1. Think up the longest sentence you can, the anti-paramedic method sentence.

2. Think about how you could shorten that sentence.

3. How many sentences of three words or less can you think of?

4. How many sentences of one word can you think of? (One-word sentences have an implied subject, such as commanding a pet to "Go." No using "Go" now!)

Activities

1. Pick a lengthy sentence from an article at random. Apply the paramedic method to condense it as much as possible without losing its main ideas.

2. Pick a lengthy sentence from your own writing. Apply the paramedic method to it.

3. Write a new sentence in which you apply the principles and style of the paramedic method from the start.

8

Sentence Boundaries

99% of grammar errors result from sentence boundary mistakes. Okay, maybe that's an exaggeration, but it's not a huge one.

The vast majority of grammar errors fall into only a few categories: sentence fragments, run-on sentences, and comma splices. (Non-native English speakers typically have more grammar struggles, but most of their errors also fall into these categories.) Fragments, run-ons, and comma splices are all sentence boundary issues.

You must understand sentence boundaries before you can mark them and avoid sentence fragments, run-ons, comma splices, and similar errors. Marking sentence boundaries also affects how readers process your sentences, or ideas, and facilitates "sentence variety," an important way that writers keep their readers' interest.

What Are Sentence Boundaries?

A sentence is a complete thought or idea. The reader or listener does not need any other information to comprehend it.

In grammar terms, a sentence is an "independent clause." A clause is a group of words. An independent clause, or group of words, does not need any additional information to make sense. It is a complete sentence, thought, or idea.

A complete sentence, thought, or idea requires four things:

- ❏ Subject / Actor

- ❏ Main Verb / Action

- ❏ Object / Acted On

- ❏ Punctuation / Marking the End

To put it another way, a complete sentence possesses the following:

- ❏ Subject (Actor) + Main Verb (Action) + Object (Acted On) + Punctuation (Marking the End)

Usually, the first three elements are stated within the sentence. You should then use appropriate punctuation to "mark the boundary" of the sentence. For instance, I used a comma after "Usually" and "For instance" to separate these transitions from the complete sentences that followed them. I used a period after "sentence" and "them" to mark the ends of those sentences.

If a sentence lacks one of the four elements above, then it also lacks the information necessary for the reader or listener to comprehend it. It is a "fragment" of a sentence rather than complete sentence, thought, or idea.

If a sentence includes multiple complete thoughts or ideas without appropriate punctuation to separate them, then the sentence "runs on" in a confusing way. A reader can process only so much information in one sentence. Run-on sentences are confusing.

Many sentence fragments (or incomplete sentences) and run-on sentences (or sentences that don't end when they should) result from incorrectly using punctuation and thus mis-marking sentence boundaries. Sometimes, punctuation may be neglected entirely. Other times, the wrong punctuation mark may be used.

A period gets used instead of a comma, and a "dependent clause" (see below) becomes a sentence fragment. A comma gets used instead of a period, and then you have a run-on sentence.

Lastly, comma splices are a special type of run-on sentence in which a comma separates two complete sentences rather than a period.

How to Mark Sentence Boundaries and Achieve Sentence Variety

Again, a complete sentence, thought, or idea consists of the following:

❑ Subject (Actor) + Main Verb (Action) + Object (Acted On) + Punctuation (Marking the End).

At the most basic level, you would use a period after each complete sentence to mark its end. But if every sentence were so simple, then your writing could become "choppy" and even mind-numbing. So-called "sentence variety" is important to maintaining readers' interest.

How can you achieve sentence variety?

❑ Combine multiple sentences into one sentence with commas and conjunctions.

❏ Add transitions or introductory phrases to the beginning of sentences.

❏ Use a comma after the transition or introductory phrase.

❏ Add lists, "dependent clauses," or "-ing verb phrases" to the endings of sentences.

❏ Use a comma before the list, dependent clause, or "-ing verb phrase."

❏ Add "dependent clauses" to the middle of sentences.

❏ Use a comma before and after the dependent clause to separate it from the rest of the sentence.

Special note: Use periods to mark the ends of complete sentences. Use commas to mark the boundary between an incomplete sentence (like a transition word) and a complete sentence.

Let's further explore each of these methods of creating sentence variety as well as the correct use of periods and commas to mark sentence boundaries.

Combine Multiple Sentences with Commas and Conjunctions

First, you can combine multiple complete sentences into one sentence by using a comma and a conjunction. There are only seven conjunctions in English, as listed below:

❑ Subject + Main Verb + Object , for Subject + Main Verb + Object.

❑ Subject + Main Verb + Object , and Subject + Main Verb + Object.

❑ Subject + Main Verb + Object , nor Subject + Main Verb + Object.

❑ Subject + Main Verb + Object , but Subject + Main Verb + Object.

❑ Subject + Main Verb + Object , or Subject + Main Verb + Object.

❑ Subject + Main Verb + Object , yet Subject + Main Verb + Object.

❑ Subject + Main Verb + Object   , so   Subject + Main Verb + Object.

Sometimes, you will see or use transition words like "however" or "therefore" between two complete sentences. You cannot use commas before them because they are not conjunctions. Instead, use a semicolon before the transition and a comma after it.

Special note: If you added a third complete sentence, then you would have a run-on sentence. Never combine more than two complete sentences with a comma and conjunction.

Add Transitions or Introductory Phrases to a Sentence's Beginning (with Commas Afterward)

Second, you can add transitions or introductory phrases to the beginning of sentences. The transition or introductory phrase could be deleted, and the rest of the sentence would still make sense. Adding these elements increases sentence variety and also helps guide readers through your ideas.

❑ [Transition] + [Comma] + Subject + Main Verb + Object.

❑ [Introductory phrase] + [Comma] + Subject + Main Verb + Object.

Adding the transition "Second" at the beginning of the prior paragraph tells readers they will read about the second technique mentioned in this section of the chapter. If I deleted it, the rest of the sentence would still contain a complete thought or idea. Thus, I used a comma to separate the transition from the complete sentence.

In the previous paragraph, I wrote the introductory phrase, "If I deleted it," as a way of contextualizing the rest of that sentence. The sentence makes more sense (I hope) because of the phrase introducing it. But that phrase could be deleted, and the sentence would still make sense to a reader or listener. Therefore, I used a comma to separate it from the sentence.

Add Lists, Dependent Clauses, or "-ING Verb Phrases" to a Sentence's Ending (with Commas Before)

Third, you can add lists, dependent clauses, or "-ing verb phrases" to the endings of sentences. You write the complete sentence like usual, and then you add on to it:

- ❏ Subject + Main Verb + Object + [Comma] + [List].
- ❏ Subject + Main Verb + Object + [Comma] + [Dependent Clause].

❑   Subject + Main Verb + Object + [Comma] + [-ing verb phrase].

In the chapter on the paramedic method, I showed how you could write a complete sentence and then add a list of supporting details or information:

❑   "Sadly, many people rely on virtual worlds, such as …."
❑   Or "Many people rely on virtual worlds, like …."
❑   Or "Many people rely on virtual worlds, including …."

If an "independent clause" is a group of words that does not need any additional information to communicate a thought or idea, then a "dependent clause" is a group of words that needs further information to make sense to a reader or listener. It "depends" on the rest of the sentence to make any sense to the reader.

A list of details added to a complete sentence is a dependent clause. Listing "email, texting, social media, and online games" by itself would not communicate a comprehensible thought or idea to the reader. The list "depends" on the rest of the sentence to make sense.

There are many other ways to add "dependent clauses" to a complete sentence.

- ❑ "Sadly, many people rely on virtual worlds, a commentary on our society's loneliness."
- ❑ "Many people rely on virtual worlds, something unimaginable only a few decades ago."
- ❑ "The War on Drugs does not deter crime, contrary to popular belief."
- ❑ "The War on Drugs increases government corruption and spending, due to fraud, waste, and mismanagement."
- ❑ "Renewable energy sources cannot provide for all of our energy needs, which means we also need nuclear power plants."

Essentially, you add a comment or detail to the end of the sentence, and you separate it from the complete sentence, thought, or idea with a comma so that readers don't accidentally blend the two things together while reading. You use the comma to help readers process what they're reading, so that they don't confuse themselves.

Also, you can write a complete sentence and then add what I call an "-ing verb phrase." Adding a verb phrase will provide more "action" to the sentence. I like using this technique to communicate that the sentence's main idea does or leads to something.

For example:

- ❑ "Sadly, many people rely on virtual worlds, seeking online connections that they perceive as safer than face-to-face relationships."

- ❑ "Many people rely on virtual worlds, showing society's evolution from only a few decades ago."

- ❑ "The War on Drugs does not deter crime, wasting taxpayer money and jailing nonviolent offenders with little benefit to society."

- ❑ "The War on Drugs increases government corruption and spending, shocking those who expected only positive outcomes from fighting drug trafficking."

Once again, use a comma to separate the complete sentence from the added "-ing verb phrase" so that readers do not get confused while reading and then have to back-track and re-read.

Add Dependent Clauses to the Middle of Sentences (with Commas Before and After)

Lastly, you can add a dependent clause to the middle of a sentence. You must separate the dependent clause from the rest of the sentence by using a comma before and after it.

For example:

- ❏ "Many people, sadly, rely on virtual worlds."
- ❏ "Many people, fearing face-to-face relationships, rely on virtual worlds."
- ❏ "The War on Drugs, contrary to popular belief, does not deter crime."
- ❏ "The War on Drugs leads to nonviolent offenders, who may be guilty only of drug possession, serving long prison sentences."

This technique can be helpful when you want to achieve a certain rhythm in your sentence. Or you may want to mix things up when you find yourself relying too much on the earlier strategies to achieve sentence variety.

> Special note: When you use phrases like "who may be guilty …," you should be careful whether you use a comma or not. If you could delete the phrase without confusing the reader, then you should use the comma with it. If you must have the phrase for the reader's comprehension, then you should not use the comma. The comma signals either the importance or lack of importance in the phrase.

For instance, "People who fear face-to-face relationships rely on virtual worlds." In this sentence, we are talking about a specific type of people, not just any people. You can't delete the phrase "People who fear ...." without confusing the reader, so do not use a comma before or after it.

Summarizing Punctuation Options

As explained above, marking sentence boundaries depends, first, on understanding them and, second, on using the correct punctuation. You can use periods, semi-colons, or commas and conjunctions to separate one complete sentence from another complete sentence. You can use commas and other punctuation marks to separate a complete sentence from an incomplete sentence. The table below summarizes your options for punctuating between complete and incomplete sentences:

Table 3. Options for Punctuating Between Complete and Incomplete Sentences

Separates Complete Sentences from Complete Sentences

Period	Semicolon (with Transition)	Comma *and* Conjunction
.	; ; therefore, ; however, etc.	, for , and , nor , but , or , yet , so

Table 3 Cont. Options for Punctuating Between

Complete and Incomplete Sentences				
Separates Complete Sentences and Incomplete Sentences				
Conjunction Alone	**Comma**	**Colon**	**Dash**	**Parentheses**
for and nor but or yet so	,	:	—	( )

Here is another way of putting it:

- ❏ Complete sentence[.] Complete sentence.
- ❏ Complete sentence[;] complete sentence.
- ❏ Complete sentence[, for] complete sentence.
- ❏ Complete sentence[, and] complete sentence.
- ❏ Complete sentence[, nor] complete sentence.
- ❏ Complete sentence[, but] complete sentence.
- ❏ Complete sentence[, or] complete sentence.
- ❏ Complete sentence[, yet] complete sentence.
- ❏ Complete sentence[, so] complete sentence.
- ❏ Complete sentence [conjunction] incomplete sentence.
- ❏ Incomplete sentence[,] complete sentence.

- ❑ Complete sentence[,] incomplete sentence.
- ❑ Start of a complete sentence[,] incomplete sentence[,] rest of the complete sentence.]

We will cover the use of colons, dashes, and parentheses in the next chapter, but I'll introduce them here along with the more standard options for marking sentence boundaries:

- ❑ Complete sentence[:] incomplete sentence (or a lengthy list).
- ❑ Complete sentence [—] incomplete sentence.
- ❑ Start of a complete sentence [—] incomplete sentence [—] rest of the complete sentence.
- ❑ Start of a complete sentence (incomplete sentence) rest of the complete sentence.
- ❑ Complete sentence (incomplete sentence).

Where Does It Fit in the Equation?

Sentence boundaries enable you to write well-structured sentences. Marking the boundaries with correct punctuation helps readers process your sentences/ideas, and they facilitate sentence variety.

We will add it under "paramedic method" in our equation:

Audience-Awareness + <u>Purpose</u> + Thesis(PEE) + CLTs + <u>PM</u> +

….

Genre

Boundaries

Here are some thought-exercises and activities to build your understanding and awareness of sentence boundaries as well as your ability to mark them.

Thought-Exercises

1. Think up the longest run-on sentence you can.

2. Now consider how to break up the run-on sentence.

3. Come up with a pair of sentences. How many ways could you combine them into one sentence, including rewriting one of the sentences to become an introductory phrase or a dependent clause?

Activities

1. Read aloud a paragraph from an article at random. Say the punctuation marks out loud ("period" and "comma" and so on). Notice how the punctuation affects how you process the sentences and their information.

2. Remove all of the punctuation from a paragraph of your writing. Read it again and notice how hard it is to understand.

3. Add punctuation back to the paragraph, but change the sentences and the punctuation so that you have different sentences with different boundaries than before.

9

A Practical Style Guide

Style refers to the customary way that an author writes. There are preferences for how authors in general write, and several best-selling books and virtually every writing textbook offer detailed descriptions of these preferences and advice for how to follow them and their general principles.

Most style guides run dozens of pages and contain a multitude of examples and nuances. They strive to turn writers into literary artists. Since I'm offering practical help to writers with practical needs, I will follow my own advice and keep it simple.

Keep It Simple

When writing to inform or persuade, the reader's focus should be on your ideas, not your sophisticated sentences and clever phrases. Keep your sentences simple so that readers can focus on content.

The simplest sentence structure consists of a subject (actor), a main verb (action), and an object that receives the action (acted on). You can add to that basic structure in many ways, as shown below. (Also see the "Sentence Boundaries" chapter.)

❑ Subject (Actor) + Main Verb (Action) + Object (Acted On) + Period (Marking the End).

❑ Smartphones connect people.

❑ Subject + Main Verb + Object + [Conjunction] + Object + Period.

❑ People value connectivity and access to information.

❑ Subject + Main Verb + Object + [Comma] + [Conjunction] + Subject + Main Verb + Object.

❑ Connectivity allows faster communication, and information enables decision-making.

❑ [Transition] + [Comma] + Subject + Main Verb + Object.

   ❑ Also, smartphones double as mini-televisions.

❑ [Introductory phrase] + [Comma] + Subject + Main Verb + Object.

   ❑ Thanks to faster mobile networks, smartphones have revolutionized what people can do on the go.

❑ Subject + Main Verb + Object + [Comma] + [List].

   ❑ Users can even upload large data files to the internet, such as pictures, video, and audio.

❑ Subject + Main Verb + Object + [Comma] + [Dependent Clause].

   ❑ Younger users record and upload billions of hours of video to YouTube, which makes it one of the most popular internet sites.

❑ Subject + Main Verb + Object + [Comma] + [-ing verb phrase].

   ❑ Smartphones decrease the barriers to recording and uploading videos, turning everyone with a smartphone into a potential filmmaker.

- ❏ Subject + [Comma] + [Dependent Clause] + [Comma] + Main Verb + Object.
- ❏ Smartphones, it is safe to say, are here to stay.

Notice that sometimes I used adjectives and additional verb phrases to flesh out the sentence's content and details. Each of these structures and examples can be built upon further. I can't provide an exhaustive list of all the possible sentence structures, but I wanted to offer some templates to illustrate building on basic sentence structure and to provide a reference for you.

If you really want to take a mathematical approach to writing, you could cycle through these sentence structures in a semi-regular pattern. One of my English professors said he cycled through about five basic sentence structures.

Short Sentences, Strong Verbs

Generally, shorter sentences are better than longer ones. Readers can get "lost" in very long sentences. They lose track of the sentence's point by the time they get to the end, and then they need to reread the whole sentence. Rarely should a sentence be longer than about thirty to thirty-five words.

A short sentence can also be "punchy." It gets to the point. It focuses.

Having said that, not all sentences must be short and punchy. You want to vary the structure and length of your sentences, or else you can numb the reader's mind. Short sentence after short sentence can make your writing seem choppy and underdeveloped. Long sentence after long sentence can be difficult and exhausting. Mix it up.

A sentence of any length should have the strongest verb possible. The verb "to be" gets singled out in the paramedic method because of its weakness. If I say "I am" or "there is," no clear meaning or image comes into the audience's mind. A strong verb brings a clear meaning and/or image to the reader's mind. To say "I pushed him" creates a different image than "I pulled him."

Consider the action in your sentence. Then choose an "action verb" that conveys the action to the reader. If you can't convey the action in an action verb, then use a verb that evokes a clear meaning for the reader. "Evokes" is certainly better than my initial thought, "has."

"Short sentences, strong verbs" is common writing advice for a reason.

Use Different Punctuation for Different Purposes

Using punctuation effectively affects how readers process information and will also correct most sentence fragments, run-on sentences, and other grammatical errors. The key is using the right punctuation mark for the right purpose.

If you used, say, a period when you should have used a comma, then you would affect how (easily) the reader processes the information and understands the sentence. If you neglected to use commas where you needed them, then readers might have difficulty separating the thoughts and ideas in your sentences, or even distinguishing sentences, and would be confused and frustrated.

Each punctuation mark represents a certain length, strength, or type of pause. Over time, writers used the same punctuation marks in the same ways, and these uses came to be regarded as "rules" writers should follow. Since writers usually follow the "rules," readers are conditioned by experience to expect certain punctuation marks to be used in certain ways.

Certain types, lengths, or "strengths" of pauses can be used to separate complete sentences from other complete sentences, while other types, lengths, or "strengths" of pauses cannot. A period is the longest, strongest pause, and it is a "full stop" after a sentence or thought.

Conversely, some lengths or "strengths" of pauses can separate incomplete sentences from complete sentences, but others cannot. A comma is the shortest, weakest pause, and it is a brief separation between a complete sentence or thought and the partial sentence or thought that goes with it.

In chapter 7, "Sentence Boundaries," I provide a table that summarizes the options for punctuating between complete sentences and separating complete and incomplete sentences. These options reflect the purposes of different punctuation marks.

Common Punctuation Errors and their Correction

Below, I will explain some of the most common errors in punctuation, how to correct them, and why the correct punctuation mark works better.

Comma Splices

A comma by itself is not a strong enough pause to separate two complete sentences or thoughts. It splices (or joins) those sentences into a type of "run-on sentence." So-called "comma splices" are easy to find with a "CTRL+F Search." Then change the comma to either a period or a semi-colon, or add a conjunction (for, and, nor, but, or, yet, so) after the comma. These three punctuation options have enough length or strength in the pause to separate two complete sentences, thoughts, or ideas in the reader's mind.

Comma Splices and Transition Words

Transition words like "however," "therefore," "instead," and so forth are not conjunctions; thus, when you place a transition word between two complete sentences, you should use a semi-colon before it and a comma after it rather than committing a comma splice. Writers sometimes use transition words similarly to conjunctions, so they must watch their punctuation around transitions vs. conjunctions between complete sentences.

Commas and Incomplete Sentences

In contrast to other options, commas are perfect for separating an incomplete sentence (or thought) from a complete sentence (or thought). A comma has the right brevity or weakness in its pause to represent the pause between an introductory phrase (like "In contrast,") and the complete sentence that follows, or the pause between a complete sentence and the added phrase after it (like ", such as ..." or ", including …").

Use Advanced Punctuation to Pack Content into Sentences

More advanced punctuation (like colons, dashes, or parentheses) can help you pack detail into a sentence without sacrificing clarity or smoothness.

It can also help you achieve certain types of pauses or shifts in thought — perhaps a dramatic pause before a word or phrase — that creates a more engaging tone in your writing "voice."

For more information, refer to the following: the "Sentence Boundaries" chapter and the table that summarizes punctuation options.

Do you see what I mean about punctuation separating sentences or ideas, structuring thought, and either facilitating or impeding one's processing of information?

In the first paragraph of this section, I demonstrated how parentheses can be used to insert a phrase into a sentence. I could have used commas, but parentheses can be less intrusive. When readers see the parentheses, their minds "down-shift" and don't read the content inside the parentheses with the same attention or emphasis as the rest of the sentence. Using parentheses tells readers to process the information inside them as less important. Parentheses are great for adding information that may be helpful but is not essential and doesn't warrant the same emphasis as surrounding information.

In the second paragraph of this section, I showed how dashes can be used to insert a phrase into a sentence. Dashes work best when there is a strong, abrupt shift in thought or tone between the rest of the sentence and the inserted phrase. Dashes tell readers that the additional information shifts to a different topic or tone.

The third paragraph of this section illustrates how a colon can be used to signal a continuation of the thought or sentence. Instead of a period, which would make "the 'Sentence Boundaries' chapter … " into a sentence fragment, I used a colon to tell the reader that the prior sentence introduced or set up the information following the colon. A colon tells the reader that the sentence's thought continues.

Using more advanced punctuation can help you pack more detail and information into a sentence without hurting your writing's clarity or making it too wordy. With practice, you will become proficient in using these different punctuation marks.

How Do I Apply All of This?

To write simple, short sentences with strong verbs, watch for lengthy sentences with overly complex structure and/or weak verbs. Then apply the paramedic method of editing to those sentences (see Chapter 6). The more you apply and practice the paramedic method, the more you will write in this style without thinking too much about it.

Additionally, even simple and short sentences may lack strong verbs. Pay special attention to the verbs in your sentences. Are you using "action verbs" that have a clear meaning or create a vivid image in the reader's mind? Could you use a stronger verb that has more emphasis?

Also pay attention to the adverbs you use. Adverbs are words that describe a verb, such as "He ran quickly." (Adverbs always end in "-ly.") Could you delete the adverb if you used a stronger verb? What about, "He sprinted" instead? Or "He fled"? Obviously, there's a difference in meaning between "sprinted" and "fled." Using a stronger verb can tease out the meaning you really wanted to convey.

To improve your use of punctuation, read your writing out loud with emphasis and feeling, the way you would want an audience to hear it. Pay attention to where you naturally pause, not where you take breaths.

Then use a comma — except between complete sentences — to represent those natural pauses, unless more advanced punctuation would be more appropriate for the type of pause you need to represent or more effective for packing detail into the sentence.

Where Does It Fit in the Equation?

Style is only part of writing well, but it is an important part. When you express ideas both clearly and correctly, then you enable readers to focus on the ideas rather than how artistically or poorly they are presented.

Style goes along with the paramedic method and sentence boundaries in our equation:

Audience-Awareness +   <u>Purpose</u>   + Thesis(PEE) + CLTs + <u>PM(Style)</u> +

Genre

Boundaries

Here are some thought-exercises and activities to develop your style and punctuation.

Thought-Exercises

1. Contemplate clever turns-of-phrase that you like. What makes them unique and engaging?

2. Who is your favorite writer, speaker, musician, or actor? What makes this person's style interesting and appealing?

3. How would you describe your writing style? What would improve it?

Activities

1. Pick a passage of your favorite author's writing, or a passage from an article at random. Describe the style and structure of the sentences. Notice how the author uses punctuation.

2. Write a paragraph in which you imitate the style and punctuation of your favorite author or a passage from an article you selected at random.

3. Write a paragraph in your own unique style and voice.

10

A Few Words about Diction

Diction, or word-choice, can affect reader comprehension and appreciation. Sometimes, the wrong word throws a kink into your ideas. Other times, the best word adds something extra to your sentence.

To make effective word-choices, you need to know about denotation, connotation, specificity vs. ambiguity, and the monetary worth of words.

Denotation vs. Connotation

Denotation is the literal dictionary definition of a word. You must choose the word that means what you intend to say.

Perhaps you don't know the word for what you want to say. I suggest thinking of similar words and then looking them up at dictionary.com or thesaurus.com. You will see definitions that may jog your mind and a list of related words that may include the word you didn't know or couldn't think of. Or you may discover an even better word.

Connotation is the figurative, metaphoric, or symbolic meaning of a word. There may be two or more words that mean what you intend to say, and you may choose one over the others because its connotation more closely matches the "mood" or tone you want to achieve.

Let's say, for instance, that you were analyzing and evaluating a potential investment for a boss or client. You determine the investment is a scam. You could write, "The investment is similar to a Ponzi scheme." Or you could opt for stronger language like, "The investment is tantamount to a Ponzi scheme."

"Similar" and "tantamount" have basically the same denotation. But tantamount has a much stronger, much more negative connotation. It is reserved for outrageous, offensive ideas.

Again, you may not be familiar with the connotation of a word. If you are uncertain, you can get a good sense of a word's connotation from its dictionary definition and examples of its use. A quick visit to dictionary.com can save embarrassment from using a word like "nubile" when you really just meant "flexible."

Specificity and Precision vs. Vagueness and Ambiguity

The more specific your word-choice, the more precise it will be. The more vague, the more ambiguous.

Specific language leaves less room for differing interpretations and understandings. Therefore, it communicates more precisely and effectively.

General, vague language opens up space for possible interpretations and thus different, conflicting understandings. It is often less precise and clear for readers.

Consider these examples of vague, ambiguous language:

- ❏ Electric vehicles are vastly superior.
    - ❏ Why are they superior?

- ❏ He's a cheater.
    - ❏ How so? Did he cheat on a test? In a game? In a financial deal? In another context?

❑ The dose is a lot.

    ❑ How much? What is a lot?

In contrast, specific language gets to the point, provides more substance, and communicates more precisely and clearly.

❑ Electric vehicles have far better fuel economy and are much more environmentally friendly.

❑ He's a con-artist.

❑ The correct dose is 100 grams.

Strive to use specific, precise word-choices to communicate most clearly.

Using Jargon (or Not)

Jargon — specialized terms that people must be familiar with to understand — can help you communicate more effectively when your audience shares your familiarity with and understanding of the jargon.

Doctors use medical jargon like "mitral valve prolapse," lawyers use phrases like "fruit of the poisoned tree," and physicists talk in arcane mathematical terms. They wouldn't use special terms if they were harder to understand. These terms facilitate communication.

For example, the phrase "process-oriented pedagogy" means very little to the average person, but it carries an immense amount of information and meaning for writing teachers like me. Think about your own job, interests, hobbies, or friendships. You use jargon and "inside references" that outsiders would not understand.

If you use jargon that the audience understands, then you can communicate more precisely and efficiently. But if your audience doesn't know the jargon, then you will lose them entirely unless you define and explain the terms. Most likely, you can (and should) choose words that your readers will already understand.

The Problem with Five-Dollar Words

So-called "five-dollar words" make a writer appear to be trying way too hard. A simpler, more common word would obviously work just as well, if not better, so the big fancy word strikes the reader as a little absurd. Contrary to the writer's intention, the five-dollar word detracts from the reader's perception of both the writing and the writer.

For example, why use a grandiose word like "sojourn" when "journey" would work just as well? Or for that matter, why use "grandiose" when "fancy" could work? Why describe someone as "apoplectic" instead of "red-faced and ranting"?

The best word very well may be the biggest, grandest, or "smartest sounding." But if there is a simpler, more common, or more vivid word with the same denotation and connotation, then choose that word by default. It will usually be more specific and precise anyway.

Commonly Confused Words

Some words are easily confused with each other. Here is a table listing and distinguishing some very commonly confused words:

Table 4. List of Commonly Confused Words		
It's Contraction of "It is"	Its Possessive Pronoun	
You're Contraction of "You are"	Your Possessive Pronoun	
They're Contraction of "They are"	Their Possessive Pronoun	There A placeholder
Two The number	To A preposition	Too Emphasizes an additional idea
Effect Noun: Results of Something (e.g., "He had a big effect.") Verb: To bring about (e.g., "He can effect change."	Affect Noun: Emotional display (e.g., "He had a flat affect.") Verb: To impact something (e.g., "He affected others."	

To avoid confusing words, use spell-check and grammar-check. These tools are helpful, but they are not foolproof. Spell-check won't catch "too" when you meant "to," for example, because they are both correctly spelled words.

Hold down the "CTRL" key and the "F" key at the same time to perform a "CTRL+F search" for words that you get confused, and then double-check how you used those specific words. Are you using the right word in the right context?

Where Does It Fit in the Equation?

Diction, or word-choice, can affect the reader's comprehension and perception of your writing. It can enhance or undercut great development, organization, and style.

Choose appropriate, effective words for what you intend to say and the "mood" you hope to create. Double-check words that you are uncertain about, saving your reader potential confusion and yourself potential embarrassment.

Our equation is nearly complete:

Audience-Awareness +   <u>Purpose</u>   + Thesis(PEE) + CLTs + <u>PM(Style)</u> + Diction + ...

Genre

Boundaries

Here are some thought-exercises and activities to improve your diction.

Thought-Exercises

1. The famous author Mark Twain said, "The right word is like lightning. The wrong word is like the lightning-bug." Consider how the word-choices in this quote make it so powerful in expressing its idea.

2. Also consider what other word-choices could work to convey the same idea with equal or greater impact.

3. What jargon could you use to communicate with co-workers, classmates, friends, or family that other groups would not understand?

Activities

1. Read a paragraph from an article at random. Notice how the word-choices affect your understanding of the writing.

2. Change some of the important words in the paragraph. Try to make them more specific and precise. Or use words with different meanings. How does the writing change as a result?

3. Pick an article or essay on a topic that you know nothing about. What kind of jargon does the author use?

4. How does the jargon affect your ability to understand the information? How does it help the audience who is familiar with it?

11

The Writing Process

Write something.

Read it.

Rewrite it.

I guarantee the rewrite will be better than the original.

When you see a book on a shelf (or in your Kindle) or an article online, you are seeing the end-result of a process. No one, not even Shakespeare, writes a perfect draft on the first try.

For this reason, the act of writing is best understood as a process. The process has five stages:

- ❑ prewriting (brainstorming ideas);
- ❑ drafting (the actual writing);
- ❑ revising (rewriting the draft);
- ❑ editing (polishing sentence structure, grammar, and punctuation); and
- ❑ proofreading (checking for typos, misspellings, and such)

While the process is described — and easily conceptualized — as linear, it is actually circular. What you revise may lead you to further brainstorming, which may then lead to more drafting, which will then require more revising. That revision could take the draft in yet another direction, adding paragraphs here and sentences there, deleting passages or phrases, or moving ideas around.

Therefore, it makes sense to brainstorm, draft, and revise the draft until you are satisfied with its content, organization, and overall effectiveness. Only then should you edit and only after editing should you proofread. You don't want to waste time editing and proofreading a draft that you may add to or cut from.

The writing process requires time. You can't write something great the hour before it's due. You must allow sufficient time for brainstorming, drafting, revising, editing, and proofreading, including breaks in between and during each stage.

What is "The One Right Answer" Again?

So, exactly how should you prewrite, draft, revise, edit, and proofread?

In other words, what is the best writing process?

Answer: the process that works best for you.

There is not a "one right answer" to the question of a writing process for everyone. There is only "the one right answer" for you.

Some people think through their entire draft before even starting. Others don't know what they want to say until they have written the draft.

Some people can't concentrate in busy public places. Others find isolation in a silent study room to be maddening.

Some people rewrite in short bursts, even while still drafting. Others put their writing away and rewrite it much later.

Writing is a process, but there are as many processes as there are people. Determine what works best for you, and devote the time and effort necessary for engaging in your process.

Below, I list and explain some of the most common and effective strategies for prewriting, drafting, revising, editing, and proofreading. Choose what works best for you. Experiment if you must. Try different strategies when you get stuck.

For example, I don't usually outline shorter pieces of writing, but I find outlines helpful when writing something longer. Yes, I know I promised "the one right answer," but when it comes to the many different writing tasks and challenges we might face, we must sometimes look for the right answer.

The lists below should help.

Prewriting (Brainstorming) Strategies

❑ Listing

    ❑ List as many ideas as you can, in no particular order. I like this strategy for coming up with a topic to write about as well as coming up with ideas about the topic that I chose.

❑ Mapping / Webbing

    ❑ Write down a topic. Circle it. Then branch off with related topics or subtopics, each in its own circle. You can branch off those, too. I also like this strategy for coming up with a topic and for developing ideas on a topic.

❏ Freewriting

    ❏ Write whatever comes to mind for three minutes, including "I have no idea what to write." The free association and the time-limit are key. Freewriting can help you overcome writer's block.

❏ Outlining

    ❏ Create an ordered, hierarchical outline of your ideas. You could use short phrases or complete sentences. Outlining helps generate ideas, but it also aids organization.

❏ Examples

    ❏ Come up with examples related to your topic or point. You can use these examples in your writing.

❏ Cause-Effect

    ❏ Write a "cause-and-effect statement" for your topic or point. If you were writing about climate change, then you might write "CO2 emissions cause the greenhouse effect" or "The effects of

Climate Change include ...." A cause-and-effect statement can help clarify a topic or generate ideas for writing.

❑ Definition

    ❑ Define your topic or something related to it. For example, "Climate change is ...." or "Love is ...." To back up your definition, you will find yourself writing quite a bit.

❑ Division / Classification

    ❑ Divide or classify your topic, or aspects of it, into categories. For instance, "Love belongs with other categories of mental disorders" or "Love can be platonic, romantic, or familial." You may also say what love is not. To back up your classifications, you will write a lot.

❑ Degree

    ❑ Consider how your topic differs from other topics in degree rather than kind. Various things can be on different points of the same continuum. If love and insanity are in the same category, then do they differ in degree of irrationality? Explain in your writing.

- ❑ Similarity / Comparison
  - ❑ Compare your topic, or aspects of it, to other topics or ideas, highlighting their similarities. For instance, "Love and insanity are both irrational." Explain in your writing.

- ❑ Difference / Contrast
  - ❑ Contrast your topic, or aspects of it, to other topics or ideas. What makes your topic different or unique? "Love is the one form of irrationality that everyone celebrates." Explain in your writing.

- ❑ Authoritative Testimony
  - ❑ What do authorities or experts say about the topic? A good Martin Luther King Jr. quote about justice will help set up your writing about justice or support your point about justice.

- ❑ Truism or "Old Saying"
  - ❑ People often use "old sayings," or truisms, about a topic. For instance, "Love conquers all." You could use such a saying to set up your writing or to support your point. You could argue against or in favor of the saying, or you could try to explore its truthfulness (or lack thereof).

- ❑ They Say — I Say

  - ❑ Similar to using an "old saying" to set up your writing, you can read or listen to what others have said about your topic ("They say") and then respond to it ("I say"). Your response may be agreement ("Yes"), disagreement ("No"), or a combination of both agreement and disagreement ("Maybe?" or "Yes to that part, but no to the other part"). You can develop your response in your writing.

- ❑ Syllogism

  - ❑ A syllogism is a logical structure: "Men are mortal. Socrates is a man. Socrates is moral." If you are writing about a complex, counter-intuitive, or controversial topic, then it may be helpful to break it down into a syllogism: "Love is emotional. Emotions are irrational. Love is irrational." You can further explain and back up the syllogism in your writing.

The table below groups brainstorming strategies according to personality preferences for extraversion or introversion.

Extraverts tend to brainstorm best by externalizing their ideas, either through talking with others or "getting ideas out" through freewriting.

Introverts tend to brainstorm best by internalizing their thought-process, such as thinking through ideas, reading others' ideas, or creating a plan or outline.

Of course, these are not rigid categories. It is simply an effort to help you determine what works best for you.

Table 5. Brainstorming Strategies Grouped by Extraversion vs. Introversion	
Extraverts	**Introverts**
Talking	Thinking
Reading	Reading
Free Writing	Planning
Listing	Outlining
Mapping	

Writing (Drafting) Strategies

❑ Choose good writing tools or methods for you.

❑ Some people prefer the tactile experience of writing with old-fashioned pen and paper. Other people prefer the speed of typing. Sometimes, I like to write on my phone because I can't type as fast and that slows down my thinking. Choose the tools or methods that best facilitate your thinking.

❑ Choose a good environment for you.

❑ Consider the When, Where, What, and Who of your writing environment

❑ When are you freshest or most energized? Are you a morning person or a night owl?

❑ What type of place stimulates your mind or fills you with energy? Do you like the outdoors? A busy coffee shop? A quiet corner or room?

❑ What do you need, or not need, in the surrounding environment to think most clearly or productively? Does some background noise help?

❑ Do you find other peoples' presence helpful or distracting? Do you like to bounce ideas off people every so often or think for long uninterrupted periods?

❑ Manage your time and energy.

❑ Plan on your writing taking some time. You might carve out some time each day, or you might devote most of a special day to a writing task.

❑ Break a large writing task into smaller pieces. Set the goal of writing the introduction by Friday. Give yourself the reward of not worrying about the writing until Monday, so you can enjoy your weekend knowing you are well on your way.

❑ Build in breaks. Taking breaks from writing helps you replenish your energy, think of new ideas, and see your writing with fresh eyes.

❑ Plan on revising multiple times, then editing multiple times, and proofreading multiple times. Don't plan on submitting your first draft. Allow ample time for multiple rounds of revision, editing, and proofreading.

❑ Apply PEE Structure as you write.

❑ Are you making a clear, purposeful point in the paragraph?

❑ Do you back up that point with relevant, legitimate, reasonable evidence?

❑ Do you explain how the evidence backs up the point and the thesis?

❑ Will the reader have any questions that you can anticipate and address before moving on to your next paragraph or point?

❑ Apply CLTs as you write.

❑ Are you repeating or restating key ideas at strategic points?

❑ Are there "related words," or contextual synonyms or antonyms, that you can use to connect ideas?

❑ Are there categories and members of those categories that you can emphasize?

❑ Can you add transitions anywhere?

❑ Pause and review your writing. Look ahead to what you plan to write next.

❏ How might it be affected by what you have written so far?

❏ Do you need to change any of it?

Rewriting (Revising) Strategies

❏ Focus on the "big picture" concerns (e.g., Is your thesis clear? Do you support it?).

❏ Leave "small picture" concerns like sentence structure and grammar for later editing.

❏ Reread multiple times, focusing on something different each time.

❏ Read from the intended reader's perspective or point-of-view.

❏ Anticipate and address the reader's questions, confusions, concerns, or objections.

❏ Double-check your draft against the assignment's requirements or expectations. Ensure that your draft "fits" the genre and fulfills the audience's expectations, needs, or goals.

❑ Identify and double-check the thesis statement, or BLUF, in your introduction. Underline the specific details in your thesis.

❑ Reverse-outline your draft to help write a stronger thesis statement or BLUF.

❑ Look to your conclusion for inspiration to write a stronger thesis statement.

❑ Outline your paragraphs' PEE structure. Improve the PEE as needed.

❑ Try to incorporate more CLTs into your paragraphs.

❑ Double-check that you are expressing the main points or ideas that you want to communicate.

❑ Are you expressing your ideas clearly, concisely, and precisely? Can you apply the paramedic method to any wordy or confusing sentence?

❑ Take breaks.

❑ Get feedback.

Editing Strategies

- ❑ Slow down.

- ❑ Refocus on style instead of content.

- ❑ Are you using strong "action" verbs?

- ❑ Are you varying the length and structure of your sentences?

- ❑ Read out loud.

- ❑ Pay attention to where you naturally pause.

- ❑ Use the appropriate punctuation to represent those pauses.

- ❑ Also pay attention to the smoothness or awkwardness of your sentences. Can you rephrase any sentences so that they read smoother?

- ❑ Read in reverse-order.

- ❑ By reading the sentences in reverse order, you will break up the flow of your writing. By breaking up your writing's flow, you can identify sentence fragments more easily.

❑ Underline/highlight each complete sentence, thought, or idea.

❑ This can help you identify sentence fragments and run-on sentences.

❑ If you struggle with mechanical issues, like possessive apostrophes, then double-check for those issues. A "CTRL+F Search" can be very helpful.

❑ Take breaks.

❑ Reread and edit multiple times.

❑ Get feedback.

Proofreading Strategies

❑ Slow down.

❑ Refocus on words instead of style.

❑ Read out loud.

❏ Pay attention to where you naturally pause.

❏ Use the appropriate punctuation to represent those pauses.

❏ Use "CTRL+F Searches" to check for comma splices and other errors.

❏ This works especially well for comma splices, but it can be used for any errors that you know you often make.

❏ Use dictionary.com to check spelling and easily confused words.

❏ Don't rely on spell-check or grammar-check.

❏ Take breaks.

❏ Reread and proofread multiple times.

❏ Get a friend's fresh eyes.

Thought-Exercises

1. What is your usual or typical writing process like from beginning to end?

2. How much time do you spend on each stage of the writing process?

3. What parts of your writing process do you need to improve? How can you do so?

4. What have people told you were strengths or weaknesses in your writing?

5. What strategies listed above could be helpful to you?

Activities

1. Write a short essay. Pay attention to your process. What's it like? How do you feel about each stage? What could you do better next time you write?

2. Repeat number one, but write a longer essay or article.

3. Experiment with some writing process strategies that you have never used before.

4. Ask friends or peers about their writing process.

12

Putting It All Together

This book endeavored to present writing as a systematic math problem. The equation is now complete.

Develop awareness of your audience: what they know and don't know about your topic; what they value and believe; and above all, what they expect, need, or want from your writing. Get to know the concrete audience to whom you will write. Understand their familiarity and knowledge with your topic and their needs and goals as readers. Imagine that audience while you draft. Bring that imagined audience to life through the writing. And remember that you have additional audiences you must also keep in mind.

Determine your purpose in communicating, and express it to your audience in an engaging way early in your writing. Ensure that your readers soon know why your writing matters and what they should take away from it. Keep your purpose in mind during your writing process, and create a clear sense of purpose throughout the writing. Make your purpose serve the reader's needs and goals, the reasons they are reading in the first place. Enable the reader to take the action that the reader wants to take or that you hope the reader will take.

Make sure you know and understand the genre in which you are writing. Fulfill the audience's expectations for that genre and the purpose of the genre. Use the genre's conventions, features, and characteristics, so that the readers recognize the genre, know it will meet their needs and goals, and don't feel tricked halfway through your writing.

Establish your writing's purpose and main idea, central claim, or "bottom-line" in a specific, detailed thesis statement early in your writing. The specific details in your thesis will establish a sense of purpose, engage the reader's interest, and foreshadow the main points of your writing. Think of your thesis as the BLUF, or bottom-line up-front, the one thing you would tell your audience if you could tell them only one thing.

Develop and support your thesis with PEE-structured paragraphs. Each paragraph's "point sentence" should relate directly back to some detail or aspect of your thesis. Each paragraph should provide "evidence" that backs up the point and thus the thesis. But don't assume that the evidence speaks for itself. The paragraph's "explanation" should tell readers how the evidence relates to, develops, or supports the point and the thesis.

Content-lexical ties enhance the organization and structure of your writing by improving cohesion or "flow." They connect new information to ideas stated earlier in the writing or that may be coming up later in the writing. These connections can be implicit and subtle or explicit and direct. Repetition, synonyms, antonyms, related words, categories and their members, and transitions all help guide readers through your writing, creating a sense of flow.

The ideas developed with PEE and structured with CLTs come across most clearly — and with the most impact — when expressed with a paramedic method style of writing, an understanding of sentence boundaries, and the use of practical style. Applying the paramedic method of editing prevents bad writing habits and facilitates clarity, concision, and precision. Marking sentence boundaries effectively avoids most grammar errors. Simple sentence structure, strong verbs, and effective punctuation get your ideas across clearly, allowing readers to appreciate them.

Diction, or word-choice, involves both audience-awareness and precision. Connotation can affect how readers perceive and interpret your ideas. Jargon can facilitate greater understanding than common terms when the audience shares your familiarity with it. Otherwise, common words and specific language communicate more precisely, effectively, and efficiently. Always double-check words when you are uncertain about their meaning or connotation.

Writing is a circular process, whether you're writing an email, a text, or a book. You must brainstorm ideas, compose a draft, and revise that draft. Your revisions may then lead to more brainstorming, drafting, and revision. Various strategies can be helpful during each stage, and you can experiment and decide which strategies work best for you. But whatever you do, allow ample time for multiple rounds of revising "big picture" issues, followed by multiple rounds of editing and proofreading.

When you perform a math equation, there is usually a standard way of doing it, and there is certainly one right answer at the end.

When you write, there are a million ways of doing it and many "answers" can be right in their own ways. But those ways of doing it and their "answers" can, and should, be arrived at through a systematic process.

Now you have the knowledge and tools to use a systematic method for writing — to write like you're doing math.

Audience-Awareness

+ Purpose divided by Genre

+ Thesis multiplied by PEE

+ CLTs

+ PM multiplied by Style, then divided by Sentence Boundaries

+ Diction

All divided by the Writing Process

=

Writing that Achieves its Intended Purpose with its Intended Audience

Combine audience-awareness, a sense of purpose, adherence to genre conventions, a clear thesis supported with PEE paragraphs, organization enhanced with CLTs, a concise and correct writing style, and effective word-choice. Put it all over the writing process, and you can produce effective writing — writing that achieves it intended purpose with its intended audience.

Thought-Exercise:

1.   What have you learned from this book?

Activity:

1.   Write an essay about what you learned from this book that will help you improve your writing.

Appendices

Three Tips for Writing to Non-Specialists

The following essay was originally published at EdgeforScholars.org.

One evening, my professor for Dissertation Seminar randomly grouped us in pairs to discuss our dissertations. A student specializing in Literature became partnered with me, a specialist in Composition and Rhetoric.

"What's your dissertation about?" I asked.

"Narrative historiography," my peer replied.

Before giving feedback on his ideas, I had to ask, "Um, what's that?"

"It uses narratology to examine literature that reimagines historical events."

"Oh. What's narratology?"

As we progress through undergrad, grad school, and doctoral programs, we travel a winding staircase that progressively narrows until only the people in our siloed specialty remain with us. We become adept at writing about narrative historiography to people who already know about it, but we forget how to discuss our research to people outside our specialties.

Grant applications, journal articles, and other publications often have broader audiences than our fellow specialists. Here are three tips for writing effectively to broader audiences.

Recognize the Curse of Knowledge

When you understand something, you have difficulty remembering what it was like to *not* understand it. This difficulty makes it harder to communicate your understanding to others who haven't obtained it yet. That's the "curse of knowledge."

Even after my classmate explained narratology, I still didn't quite get narrative historiography until he used the example of Michael Chabon's *The Yiddish Policemen's Union*. It's a detective novel set in an alternate reality in which the Jewish nation-state resides in part of Alaska rather than in Israel. A hard-boiled detective investigates a murder and discovers a secretive group working to bring about the Messianic events required for a Jewish state in the Middle East.

Ooohhh! So "narrative historiography" is jargon for "how we tell stories about alternate reality and history." Why didn't you just say that? Because of the curse of knowledge.

To write clearly to non-specialists, you must be aware of the curse of knowledge. Remember there was a time when you didn't understand your discipline like you do now. Remember that your audience may not understand it, think about how you came to grasp it, and adjust your communication to help them get it, too.

Hunt for Threshold Concepts and Jargon

The term "threshold concept" was coined by Jan Meyer and Ray Land. A threshold concept is a counter-intuitive idea that must be understood before you can fully understand other important concepts in a given discipline. A threshold concept transforms your views of discipline-specific content. Meyer and Land describe it as a "portal" to a new way of thinking. Often, we use jargon to name or describe threshold concepts.

For example, before you can understand "narrative historiography" as a concept in the field of Literature, you first need to understand that literature can be analyzed with a range of different paradigms, all grounded to varying degrees in the details of the text and the author. Once you realize literary analysis doesn't make stuff up out of thin air, your view of literary analysis transforms.

To understand how CRISPR works, you need to understand DNA, RNA, and viruses. But when Jennifer Doudna explains CRISPR to lay-people, she doesn't take it for granted that people share her deep understanding of genetics. She doesn't use jargon like "gRNA," "tracer RNA," and "sgRNA." Instead, she describes CRISPR as "cut-and-paste" and then walks her audience through some basic threshold concepts about DNA replication.

To mitigate the curse of knowledge in your writing, look for the threshold concepts and jargon whose understanding you take for granted. Then explain those concepts in more detail, using broadly familiar language, examples, and analogies.

Pretend You're Writing to a New Grad Student

Of course, you can't over-correct when writing to the non-specialists reading your grant application, journal article, or other publication. If you start explaining the scientific method to scientists, then you'll offend your audience.

Imagine you're writing to a new graduate student in your discipline. The student understands a lot about the discipline, but the student may not have achieved the threshold concepts, higher-level jargon, and paradigms that inform you as a PhD.

My classmate, for instance, didn't need to explain the concept of using specific theories and paradigms in literary analysis (e.g., historical criticism, psychological criticism, etc.). I got that in undergrad. But he needed to explain higher-level concepts that hadn't been part of either my Masters or my Doctorate in Composition and Rhetoric.

By pretending you're writing to a new grad student, you can strike the balance between condescending to the audience and explaining what needs to be explained, between dumbing down your writing and providing the necessary details.

Example

Say you're writing an NIH grant to fund research into neural trajectory representation. The reviewers will likely include fellow neurobiologists, neurologists, and neuroscientists. But will any of them specialize in continuous cortical signals, bioengineering, neural prostheses, or robotics? Will any of them understand directional tuning and population-based movement representation in the motor cortex?

To communicate about neural trajectory representation to these relative non-specialists, recognize the curse of knowledge, identify the threshold concepts and jargon that need to be explained, and pretend you're explaining them to a brand-new doctorate student.

Using these tips, you might write something like the following:

"Researching the neuronal connections in the motor cortex that fire when we move some part of our bodies could help bioengineers develop robotic prostheses that can be controlled with the mind. Neuronal firing in the motor cortex creates a neural 'representation' of the direction and speed of volitional movements. People can imagine volitional movements, creating the neuronal firing that leads to neural representation of trajectory. If connected neurally to robotic prostheses, imagining movements enables people to control the prostheses with their minds."

Instead of throwing around "neural trajectory representation" and "continuous cortical signals" like everyone knows those concepts, remember that you didn't always know them yourself and that people outside your narrow speciality likely don't know them either. Recognize the curse of knowledge.

To explain "neural trajectory representation," you need to identify it as a threshold concept and explain it with the detail necessary for passing through the portal to a new understanding. Describing neuronal firing in the motor cortex allows you to explain that this firing creates a "representation" of both direction and speed, i.e., trajectory. Then references to "trajectory" in the context of neurobiology will make sense to neurobiologists with different specialties.

But the example doesn't condescend by defining neurons, neuronal connections, neuronal firing, or the motor cortex. The neuroscientists and bioengineers reviewing the grant may not share your narrow specialty, but they still know a thing or two. Pretending they're new grad students helps you explain what they need explained without over-explaining, offending, and wasting their time.

Conclusion

Influential literacy theorist Walter Ong says it's essential to know what the audience knows and doesn't know. That's how writers know what to explain and what to assume.

Don't let the curse of knowledge mislead you about what the audience knows and doesn't know. Look for the threshold concepts and jargon that should be explained so your readers grasp what you're trying to convey. Pretend you're writing to a new grad student so you don't over-explain.

It will avoid awkward confusion and questions about narratology, sgRNA, and neural trajectories.

Making Writing More Memorable and Persuasive

The following essay was originally published at EdgeforScholars.org.

In the last week, you've reviewed a couple hundred grant proposals. Or skimmed a couple hundred CVs and cover letters. Or graded a hundred papers. Which proposal will you advocate for? Which candidate will you pound the table to interview? Which student will you write an enthusiastic recommendation for when asked two years later?

Probably the most memorable one.

To act on information, it needs to be in long-term memory so that it's accessible when needed and can exert a lasting, formative impact.

Sure, you can always reread or look something up, but compelling communication sticks with you. It resides among the long-term memories that make you *you*, influencing your perspective, attitudes, and beliefs.

Schema theory can help you achieve compelling, influential memorability in your grant proposals, scholarly articles, and other writing.

A Ghost Story Reveals How Memory Uses Schema

Schema theory dates to Sir Frederick Bartlett's seminal work, *Remembering*.

In one of several studies he recounts, Bartlett had white, middle-class British subjects read and then recall a Native American ghost story. Invariably, they added, deleted, exaggerated, or downplayed various details. Yet they insisted they recalled the story as it was written.

Significantly, the British participants changed the culturally unfamiliar details and replaced them with more familiar versions. Some people went so far as to take the ghost out of the ghost story! When questioned about their recollections, the subjects insisted they were recalling the story as it was originally told. Bartlett realized that their memories weren't faulty; rather, human memory is *reconstructive*: we reconstruct events and information in the process of recalling them.

So-called "memory gaffes," such as Brian Williams embellishing a story of his war journalism the more he retold it, become much more explicable and innocent when we realize that people often (re)combine experiences and information from various sources into a new memory so unified that we can't disentangle which information came from which source.

Our reconstructions often involve schemata, or organized conceptual frameworks, that help structure and facilitate our cognition. Bartlett's British subjects lacked schemata for details specific to Native American culture, so their reconstructions of the ghost story transformed those details so that they fit into their existing schemata. Brian Williams' schemata probably included the danger of getting shot down by a missile and stories of other helicopters meeting that fate.

In a widely-cited study, Elizabeth Loftus demonstrated that people overestimate the speed of cars in a traffic accident if an interviewer asks, "How fast were the cars going when they *smashed* into each other?" as opposed to verbs like "hit" or "collided." Some people even recalled broken glass on the pavement even though there was none!

The word "smashed" affected the subjects' reconstruction of the accident. "Smashed" activated a different schema for car accidents than, say, "bumped." Many similar misinformation studies have confirmed memory's reconstructive, malleable nature.

If memory is reconstructive, then communication can either facilitate or impede effective, accurate reconstruction.

High School Flyers and Self-Schema Filters

We have schemata for all manner of things, including ourselves. A "self-schema" can be described as an organized conceptual framework about oneself. For an NIH study section member, it might include a combination of physician, infectious disease specialist, experienced collaborator with radiologists and engineers, and eagerness to support projects that propose unique uses of radiologic techniques and equipment in the setting of infectious disease.

Our senses are bombarded by countless stimuli per second, and self-schemata filter those stimuli so that we pay attention only to what's important. Self-schemata affect whether we notice something, how much attention we pay to it, and whether we try to encode it into long-term memory.

I asked twenty people, ten teachers and ten students, to walk down a high school hallway and report the flyers and posters they recalled. Theoretically, everyone should have remembered the flyers and posters with certain memorable characteristics, such as colorful imagery. This happened, but more commonly, the subjects' <u>self-schemata determined what they remembered</u>.

Both the teachers and students remembered things that were relevant to their self-schemata. The teachers primarily remembered flyers about upcoming school club meetings or ACT exam dates in case their students asked. The students mainly remembered posters and flyers that connected with their identities.

As the lone subject who noticed a flyer about a gun raffle said, "I noticed and remembered it because I'm a hunter, and I'd like to win a new deer rifle."

How Schema Make Information Memorable

Schema create memorability in (at least) two ways:

- Engaging Existing Schema for the Topic
- Engaging Relevant Self-Schema

In *Made to Stick*, Chip and Dan Heath capture how schemata can make information easier to understand and more memorable. You could explain a pomelo in technical detail, the Heaths say, by describing its size, shape, color, texture, etc. Or you could say that it's like a grapefruit.

We form schema to facilitate cognition and memory, so we naturally update and refine them when we learn new information. The audience can easily update their schema for grapefruit to include pomelos as similar fruit, rather than the more difficult task of creating a brand new schema for pomelos.

Your audience will almost always have existing schemata for the topic at hand. If you can activate those schemata and help the audience incorporate new information into them, then your communication will be much more memorable and effective.

To be most memorable and compelling, you can also activate the audience's self-schema. Your information will pass through the audience's attentional filter and connect with them personally and emotionally.

Example of Making Information Memorable

Unless they've recently emerged from filming a reality TV show, current readers will be well-acquainted with COVID-19, social distancing, contact tracing, testing, and vaccine development. They may or may not be familiar with using specific UV wavelengths to kill bacteria and viruses without harming human tissue, sanitizing occupied rooms.

To make a proposal for NIH funding to test the efficacy of narrow-wavelength UV light more memorable and compelling, you might write something like the following:

A vaccine's ultimate purpose is to safeguard society through herd immunity. Yet herd immunity against COVID-19 will be elusive due to unequal vaccine distribution, the anti-vaxxing movement, and SARS-CoV-2 mutations. We propose to test whether novel short-wavelength UV light can effectively kill viruses and sanitize public spaces, offices, homes, clothing, groceries, and household items without affecting human eyes, skin, or other tissues. If successful, this novel technology can help secure public health and economic reopening regardless of vaccine production, distribution, or compliance.

The opening sentence activates the NIH reviewer's self-schema as a medical expert. It screams professional relevance while also appealing to the personal desire to help people. It aims to make the reviewer nod in agreement. Pushing through the attentional filter of self-schema, the sentence ensures full attention and connects emotionally.

The next sentences tap into existing schemata implying reams of information about attaining herd immunity and resuming normal-ish life. They also help the reviewer incorporate the proposed technology into existing schemata for killing viruses and disinfecting public spaces, etc., imagining how it could work and how impactful it could be.

For more advice on aligning your grant application with organizational values, read my post on <u>audience-based rhetoric</u>. Go ahead and open a new tab. The conclusion isn't going anywhere.

Conclusion

Giving some thought to your audience's self-schema can help your writing stand out and "stick" with readers. Try to appeal to the readers' images of themselves and to ground new ideas in existing, familiar concepts.

Tapping into existing schemata for your topic can help you communicate more clearly, efficiently, and memorably. And memorable communication can influence future judgments, decisions, and actions.

How a Jail-house Letter and Goat Research Can Get Your Grant Funded

The following essay was originally published at EdgeforScholars.org.

In FY2018, NIH received nearly 55,000 grant applications and funded just over 11,000, a 20% success rate. The NSF gets about 40,000 applications a year and also funds about 11,000. Many great research proposals are left unfunded each year.

To give your grant application its best chance, ground the proposal's persuasive appeals in the values of the granting organization and its reviewers. So-called "audience-based rhetoric" persuades much more effectively than just stating the reasons your grant is the best idea ever.

MLK's Jail-House Letter: Audience-Based Rhetoric

Martin Luther King, Jr.'s "Letter from Birmingham Jail" is a classic example of using an audience's values to persuade them. The letter responded to a group of white clergymen who said that participants in the 1963 Birmingham bus boycotts should follow laws (specifically, an ordinance against marching without a permit) rather than practice civil disobedience.

Among his other arguments, King pointed out that the Boston Tea Party was an act of civil disobedience, that the founders of the United States had refused to follow unjust laws, and that Nazi Germany required reporting Jews and penalized sheltering them. Imagine those American clergymen reading their values thrown back at them but still insisting on adhering to Jim Crow!

Of course, you must get to know your audience's values before you can appeal to them.

Getting to Know Your Grant Proposal's Audience

When you read the RFA and other advice for applicants, don't only pay attention to requirements, deadlines, and details. Also look for the values espoused by the organization.

Consider some of the questions that NIH poses about a project's significance when explaining what reviewers look for:

Does the project address an important problem or *a critical barrier to progress* in the field? … How will successful completion of the [project's] aims … *drive* this field? (emphasis added)

Your research addresses a very important problem — in your eyes. But from the NIH reviewer's perspective, is your important problem a "critical barrier to progress in the field?" Will your project, if successful, "drive" the field forward? In other words, does your project support NIH's values?

Appealing to Your Grant Proposal's Audience

Audience-based rhetoric doesn't mean that you insert phrases like, "My project addresses a critical barrier to progress" or "Successful completion will drive my field," and declare your persuasive work done. It means crafting your research methods and proposal with the audience's values in mind.

Say you want to develop a machine that can run dozens of tests on a single drop of blood, without getting all Elizabeth Holmes about it. If you argue that your project merits funding because the new test will make phlebotomy less painful, then you're stating why *you* think the project is great. But you're not relating your project and its outcomes to NIH's values.

Instead, you might argue that the ability to run numerous tests on a minimal amount of blood will open new vistas of medical research, dramatically increase the efficiency and quality of medical care, usher in an era of routine blood testing, facilitate early diagnoses, catch more preventable illnesses, *and* make phlebotomy less painful. (No wonder Theranos was a thing.)

For any grant application, you must demonstrate that your project both aligns with and achieves the granting organization's values. Maybe your project has more modest goals than influencing an entire field, but you should still present it as "driving" your field forward if you want NIH's money.

Goat Research as Audience-Based Rhetoric

Goat research may seem like an odd example of presenting a (modest) proposal as if it "drives" a field, but hopefully, it will lodge as firmly in your memory as the following story stuck in mine.

Eleven years ago, I attended a graduate research symposium where a grad student listed catheterizing goats as one of her research project's most significant results. I was baffled until she contrasted her method of obtaining urine samples with the standard, inhumane method of suffocating goats until they urinated!

Still, I wondered why goats were worth researching, why anyone should care about their urine samples. If that grad student were applying for an NIH grant to analyze goat urine, I'm sure the reviewers would have similar questions.

In answer, the applicant could write something like the following:

> Testing goat urine for biomarkers associated with antibiotics has the potential for three significant impacts on the fields of animal science, agriculture, and nutrition science. First, detecting excessive amounts of these biomarkers would indicate possible health impacts on livestock and from consuming livestock. Completing the research would also demonstrate how a new, more humane method of urine collection can be used on other livestock and similar animals.

> Future researchers in animal science, agriculture, and other fields would be able to conduct more ethical research on animals, in accordance with the PHS Policy on Humane Care and Use of Laboratory Animals and NIH's guidance to "avoid or minimize animal discomfort, distress, and pain." This proposed research would create new norms for animal research

sponsored by NIH, which would then spread to other institutions and advance the ethics of all animal research.

This example aligns with several of NIH's values by presenting the research as propelling multiple fields (animal science, agriculture, and nutrition science) with both new knowledge (antibiotic levels) and innovative methods (catheterizing goats). It also frames the new, more humane method of collecting goat urine as supporting NIH's explicitly stated value on minimizing animal discomfort and its implicit value of shaping fields and methods of research.

The example argues that the research could turn up nothing about antibiotic levels yet still serve NIH's values, goals, and purposes by transforming the methods and ethics of animal research, thus positioning NIH as a powerful influence on future research regardless of the project's findings.

Even something as esoteric as catheterizing goats can come across as a potential game-changer when it aligns with the audience's values.

Conclusion

Identifying and using the audience's values will help you develop arguments that not only persuade but also excite reviewers to recommend your research project. Carefully review the RFP for the granting organization's explicit and implicit values and build them into how you describe your research. Especially the goat research.

References

Ede, Lisa and Andrea Lunsford. "Audience Addressed/Audience Invoked: The Role of Audience in Composition Theory and Pedagogy." College Composition and Communication, 1984.

Reiff, Mary Jo. "Rereading 'Addressed' and 'Invoked' Readers Through a Social Lens: Toward a Recognition of Multiple Audiences." JAC: Journal of Advanced Composition, 1996.

Lanham, Richard. Revising Prose. 4th Edition. Allyn and Bacon, 2000.

Liu, Dilin. "Writing Cohesion: Using Content-Lexical Ties in ESOL." English Teaching Forum, 2000.

Follow the Author

Eric Sentell writes about faith, politics, relationships, writing, and media and other impolite topics on Medium at ericsentell.medium.com.

Eric also writes a newsletter featuring advice for communicating and round-ups of some "feel-good" positive news stories to help brighten the start of each month. Sign up here.

His work has appeared at Edge for Scholars, the peer-reviewed journals Technical Communication and Relevant Rhetoric, and in various literary journals.

If you enjoyed this book, you'll also like Become Your Own Fact-Checker: Know Who's Misleading and Manipulating You.

Like Eric's author page on Facebook
Follow Eric on Twitter @Eric_Sentell
Follow Eric on LinkedIn @EricSentell